Shakespeare and Ecocritical Theory

ARDEN SHAKESPEARE AND THEORY

Series Editor: Evelyn Gajowski

AVAILABLE TITLES

Shakespeare and Economic Theory David Hawkes
Shakespeare and Ecocritical Theory Gabriel Egan
Shakespeare and Psychoanalytic Theory Carolyn Brown

FORTHCOMING TITLES

Shakespeare and Cultural Materialist Theory
Christopher Marlow
Shakespeare and Ecofeminist Theory Rebecca Laroche
and Jennifer Munroe
Shakespeare and Feminist Theory Marianne Novy
Shakespeare and Film Theory Scott Hollifield
Shakespeare and New Historicist Theory Neema Parvini
Shakespeare and Posthumanist Theory Karen Raber
Shakespeare and Queer Theory Melissa Sanchez

Shakespeare and Ecocritical Theory

Gabriel Egan

Bloomsbury Arden Shakespeare
An imprint of Bloomsbury Publishing Plc

B L O O M S B U R Y
LONDON • NEW DELHI • NEW YORK • SYDNEY

Bloomsbury Arden Shakespeare

An imprint of Bloomsbury Publishing Plc

Imprint previously known as Arden Shakespeare

50 Bedford Square	1385 Broadway
London	New York
WC1B 3DP	NY 10018
UK	USA

www.bloomsbury.com

BLOOMSBURY, THE ARDEN SHAKESPEARE and the Diana logo are trademarks of Bloomsbury Publishing Plc

First published 2015

© Gabriel Egan, 2015

Gabriel Egan has asserted his right under the Copyright, Designs and Patents Act, 1988, to be identified as author of this work.

British Library Cataloguing-in-Publication Data
A catalogue record for this book is available from the British Library.

ISBN:	HB:	978-1-4411-4552-9
	PB:	978-1-4411-9930-0
	ePDF:	978-1-4411-4252-8
	ePub:	978-1-4411-7824-4

Library of Congress Cataloging-in-Publication Data
Egan, Gabriel.
Shakespeare and ecocritical theory / Gabriel Egan.
pages cm-- (Shakespeare and theory ; volume 3)
Includes bibliographical references and index.
Includes webliography.
ISBN 978-1-4411-4552-9 (hardback)– ISBN 978-1-4411-9930-0 (paperback)
1. Shakespeare, William, 1564-1616–Knowledge–Natural history. 2. Ecocriticism I. Title.
PR3039.E45 2015
822.3'3–dc23
2015014056

Series: Shakespeare and Theory, 1234567X, volume 3

Typeset by Fakenham Prepress Solutions, Fakenham, Norfolk NR21 8NN
Printed and bound in Great Britain

CONTENTS

SERIES EDITOR'S PREFACE

'Asking questions about literary texts – that's literary criticism. Asking "Which questions shall we ask about literary texts?" – that's literary theory.' So goes my explanation of the current state of English studies, and Shakespeare studies, in my never-ending attempt to demystify, and simplify, theory for students in my classrooms. Another way to put it is that theory is a systematic account of the nature of literature, the act of writing, and the act of reading.

One of the primary responsibilities of any academic discipline – whether in the natural sciences, the social sciences, or the humanities – is to examine its methodologies and tools of analysis. Particularly at a time of great theoretical ferment, such as that which has characterized English studies, and Shakespeare studies, in recent years, it is incumbent upon scholars in a given discipline to provide such reflection and analysis. We all construct meanings in Shakespeare's texts and culture. Shouldering responsibility for our active role in constructing meanings in literary texts, moreover, constitutes a theoretical stance. To the extent that we examine our own critical premises and operations, that theoretical stance requires reflection on our part. It requires honesty, as well. It is thereby a fundamentally radical act. All critical analysis puts into practice a particular set of theoretical premises. Theory occurs from a particular standpoint. There is no critical practice that is somehow devoid of theory. There is no critical practice that is not implicated in theory. A common-sense, transparent encounter with any text is thereby impossible. Indeed, to the extent that theory requires us to question anew that with which

we thought we were familiar, that which we thought we understood, theory constitutes a critique of common sense.

Since the advent of postmodernism, the discipline of
English studies has undergone a seismic shift. And the
discipline of Shakespeare studies has been at the epicentre
of this shift. Indeed, it has been Shakespeare scholars who
have played a major role in several of the theoretical and
critical developments (e.g. new historicism, cultural materialism, presentism) that have shaped the discipline of English
studies in recent years. Yet a comprehensive scholarly analysis
of these crucial developments has yet to be done, and is
long overdue. As the first series to foreground analysis of
contemporary theoretical developments in the discipline of
Shakespeare studies, *Arden Shakespeare and Theory* aims to
fill a yawning gap.

To the delight of some and the chagrin of others, since
1980 or so, theory has dominated Shakespeare studies. *Arden
Shakespeare and Theory* focuses on the state of the art at the
outset of the twenty-first century. For the first time, it provides
a comprehensive analysis of the theoretical developments that
are emerging at the present moment, as well as those that are
dominant or residual in Shakespeare studies.

Each volume in the series aims to offer the reader the
following components: to provide a clear definition of a
particular theory; to explain its key concepts; to trace its major
developments, theorists, and critics; to perform a reading of a
Shakespeare text; to elucidate a specific theory's intersection
with or relationship to other theories; to situate it in the
context of contemporary political, social, and economic developments; to analyse its significance in Shakespeare studies;
and to suggest resources for further investigation. Authors
of individual volumes thereby attempt to strike a balance,
bringing their unique expertise, experience, and perspectives
to bear upon particular theories while simultaneously fulfilling
the common purpose of the series. Individual volumes in the
series are devoted to elucidating particular theoretical perspectives, such as cultural materialism, ecocriticism, ecofeminism,

economic theory, feminism, film theory, new historicism, posthumanism, psychoanalysis, and queer theory.

Arden Shakespeare and Theory aims to enable scholars, teachers, and students alike to define their own theoretical strategies and refine their own critical practices. And students have as much at stake in these theoretical and critical enterprises – in the reading and the writing practices that characterize our discipline – as do scholars and teachers. Janus-like, the series looks forward as well as backward, serving as an inspiration and a guide for new work in Shakespeare studies at the outset of the twenty-first century, on the one hand, and providing a retrospective analysis of the intellectual labour that has been accomplished in recent years, on the other.

To return to the beginning: what is at stake in our reading of literary texts? Once we come to understand the various ways in which theory resonates with not only Shakespeare's texts, and literary texts, but the so-called 'real' world – the world outside the world of the mind, the world outside the world of academia – then we come to understand that theory is capable of powerfully enriching not only our reading of Shakespeare's texts, and literary texts, but our lives.

Evelyn Gajowski
University of Nevada, Las Vegas

Introduction: Done and Undone

It is entirely possible that humans' production of atmospheric carbon dioxide gas (CO_2), mainly by the burning of fossil fuels, will soon substantially warm the Earth and change its climate. This possibility is the political and social reality at the heart of today's ecological politics, dwarfing all the other, related, fears that also traditionally come under the umbrella of ecological concern, or environmentalism. These other concerns include: the welfare of animals, especially where their usual habitats are being encroached upon by people; the effect on the landscape of industrial activities such as mining, hydrofracturing (that is, fracking) and building construction; the effect on human food of industrial farming practices, including the spraying of crops with pesticides and the injection of livestock with drugs; and pollution of the natural world in general.

In the past thirty years, the study of English Literature – within which the study of Shakespeare is an archetypal activity – has been transformed by critics converting political and social concerns into schools of critical interpretation. The feminist politics of the 1960s and 1970s generated schools of feminist literary criticism, divided along various lines arising from differences over philosophical distinctions such as essentialism and materialism. The politics of gay liberation in the 1970s and 1980s – now commonly perceived as a collective struggle against the oppression of Lesbian, Gay, Bisexual and Transgender (LGBT) people – generated a critical school of queer theory. There has been a long-standing Marxist approach to studying English Literature, and since the 1980s a number of this school's tenets have become orthodoxy within university departments of English even where (as in America) the political corollaries of Marx's ideas were not generally adopted.[1] The political and social concerns of environmentalism – broadly equivalent to ecopolitics and Green activism – have recently followed this pattern in creating a school of ecocriticism to which this book is intended as a guide.

The politicizing of literary criticism since the 1960s has generated a negative reaction, or backlash, within academic studies, to some extent arising from a belief that politics has no place within literary studies, and to some extent, less straightforwardly, arising from the symbiotic relationship within university English departments between an embedded left-wing orthodoxy and the growing acceptance of predominantly French Literary Theory. The backlash against political criticism in general is typified by Harold Bloom's excoriation of what he calls the 'Schools of Resentment';[2] this characterizes the motivation of feminists, gays and socialists not as the rational rejection of social injustice but rather as personal discontentment arising from the misfortune of being born female, homosexual or poor. The backlash against French Literary Theory is typified by three books written by Raymond Tallis,[3] and by Brian Vickers' account of the harm that Theory in general does to Shakespearian criticism.[4] The overtly political intention of the newest school, ecocriticism, is just as susceptible as its recent predecessors to the critiques of Bloom, Tallis and Vickers.

A common response to such critiques is to claim that the desire to keep politics and/or Literary Theory out of literary criticism is insincere and hypocritical, since to claim that literary criticism can be apolitical or non-theoretical is itself a political or theoretical assertion. Terry Eagleton popularized this response by citing the economist J. M. Keynes' view that 'those economists who disliked theory, or claimed to get along better without it, were simply in the grip of an older theory'.[5] Worse, it may be that declaring oneself to be apolitical or non-theoretical is merely to camouflage one's politics or theories, passing them off as uncontroversial common sense. For those who proclaim themselves to be political and theoretical, attempting to pass off political and theoretical ideas as common sense is the work done by the complex political and psychological phenomenon that is known as ideology.[6]

A straightforward response to the backlash against politicized criticism would be to call the reaction a flight from reality, for, if environmentalists are right, the end of the world as we know it really is nigh. The qualification 'if environmentalists are right ...' is needed because the deniers and minimizers of climate change are correct to assert that we do not know just how harmful in the future the consequences of our present greenhouse gas emissions will turn out to be. Taking immediate action to decrease sharply human emissions of carbon dioxide in the near future would be expensive, and opponents of such action argue that we ought not to waste resources on trying to mitigate an uncertain threat when they might better be spent elsewhere in improving human well-being, for instance, by growing the industrial economies of developing nations in order to raise their populations out of poverty. Those who hold this view think that if we do nothing to limit greenhouse gas emissions we will in a happier future look back on the early twenty-first century and be glad that we took no precipitate, unnecessary and wasteful action.

Shakespeare repeatedly dramatized his characters imagining a future in which they look back at their present state to smile upon its unseen good fortune and at the unfounded anxieties that haunted it. The earliest example, first performed in 1592 or 1593, is Hastings' response to Catesby's news that Richard Gloucester wants Hastings to lend his support to Richard's attempt to gain the throne. 'I will not do it, to the death,' exclaims Hastings, before a more cheery anticipation: 'But I shall laugh at this a twelvemonth hence' (*Richard III*, 3.2.52–4). Such anticipated retrospections are always ironic in Shakespeare, since we know (or soon learn) that the character indulging in this anticipation will not live to look back in joy.

Indeed, the wit of Shakespeare's complex construction here is that their expectation of being publicly celebrated is thwarted by that very expectation, which is itself an unflattering portrayal of them.

Shakespeare was well aware that the anticipation of a future in which the present will be remembered with pride is itself a rhetorical act in the present and is useful to bolster flagging morale and impel people to action that they would otherwise not take. In *Julius Caesar*, Cassius' speech has this as a subsidiary function, its main dramatic purpose being to allow the audience to contrast the anticipated future performance with the execution of it that they are watching. In *Henry V*, on the other hand, Shakespeare made the future from which the present is recollected be the old ages of the characters concerned rather than the 'many ages hence' when the play was first performed. Thus King Harry in his Saint Crispin's Day speech (*Henry V*, 4.3.40–67) offers his soldiers the tempting promise of future bragging rights earned by their actions in the forthcoming Battle of Agincourt. Looked at this way, his army being composed of so few is itself an advantage since: 'If we are marked to die, we are enough / To do our country loss; and if to live, / The fewer men, the greater share of honour' (*Henry V*, 4.3.20–22). This suggests that the outcome of the battle is predestined rather than being affected by the relative sizes of the armies that fight.

Thus there is more to Shakespeare's use of anticipated retrospection than mere ironic pessimism, for his plays explore the question of whether their outcomes are inevitable or merely what we call contingent, brought about by accident or avoidable human actions. In *Romeo and Juliet*, the non-delivery of Friar Laurence's letter to Romeo in Mantua is what a lawyer would call the proximate cause of the disaster. It is clear from the Friar's long recitation of events at the close of the play that he thinks his culpability extends to other reckless actions that would be categorized in legal circles as *but-for* causes: had he not supplied Juliet's coma-inducing drug, had he not secretly married her to Romeo – and so on. Yet the play's Prologue pointedly calls them 'star-crossed lovers' (Prologue.6), and Romeo says, in response to hearing of Juliet's death, 'I defy you, stars' (5.1.24), as if cosmic fatedness and not human contingency were the cause of the play's 'misadventured piteous overthrows' (Prologue.7).

In his history plays, Shakespeare extensively explored the tensions between such competing explanations for disaster. E. M. W. Tillyard sees the entire eight-play collection as a consciously conceived cycle intended to dramatize the descent into eighty-five years of a civil war occasioned by divine displeasure at the usurpation and murder of Richard II, and ended only by the ascension of Henry VII after he defeated Richard III at Bosworth Field.[7] That is, Tillyard sees the plays telling the Tudor Myth, the story by which the ruling English dynasty accounted for the general well-being of England under Queen Elizabeth, itself the sign of a divine, approving providence. The striking omission from Tillyard's model of a self-satisfied political orderliness that was thought to mirror the orderliness of the wider cosmos is the period's much-debated pragmatic doctrine of Machiavellianism. Philip Brockbank points out that this countervailing explanation for political strife and its avoidance was already present in the prose chronicle sources plundered by writers of English history plays.[8] Shakespeare's history plays can best be seen not simply as dramatizations of providential or Machiavellian accounts of England's recent past but as dramatizations of the conflicts between these expositions, as characters variously attribute to God's intervention, mischance, human foibles or Fate the historical events they are experiencing.

A complication, then, in evaluating Shakespeare's ironic use of anticipated retrospection is his refusal to settle upon a single cause of disasters, his refusal to give just one *but-for* explanation. Indeed, his characters and plays seem obsessed with exploring multiple explanations for what happens in the plays. They pay special attention to the possibility of symmetry in human affairs, pondering just how things would look from an opposite perspective, asking whether any particular phenomenon would look different if placed the other way round, and exploring the consequences of one person and another switching places. In the early plays, *The Comedy of Errors* and *The Taming of the Shrew*, this took the form of characters being mistaken for one another either by error or because of deliberate impersonation. Although Shakespeare continued to use disguise, he gave up the deliberate switching of two identities in impersonation, except for the special case of the bed-tricks in *Measure for Measure* and *All's Well that Ends Well*. The hypothetical substitution of persons remained a constant theme of his plays nonetheless. What difference does it make, the plays ask, if Hermia marries Demetrius rather than Lysander, and Helena takes whoever is left over (*A Midsummer Night's Dream*)? What difference does it make if Rosalind pretends to be a boy who pretends to be a girl who loves Orlando, rather than being that girl herself (*As You Like It*)? Or, similarly, Viola's deception of Orsino (*Twelfth Night*)? What difference does it make if Angelo stands in for the Duke, or if he is given Barnadine's head for Claudio's, or Raguzine's for Barnadine's (*Measure for Measure*)? The examples may be multiplied many times.

These are explorations of symmetry in human affairs, and, overwhelmingly, the conclusion the plays seem to reach is that gender is quite irrelevant: persons may stand in for one another without the structure of human affairs being much perturbed. Even the transition from one monarch to the next does not make much difference, despite the courtiers' fears: '[PRINCE HARRY] This is the English not the Turkish court; / Not Amurath an Amurath succeeds, / But Harry Harry' (*Henry IV, Part Two*, 5.2.47–9). The implicit contrast to such smooth succession would be a leap into the unknown of republicanism, which according to Andrew Hadfield is the always-present alternative to business as usual in Shakespeare's plays.[9]

Yet, in stark contrast to the principle of symmetry in social relations, Shakespeare repeatedly dramatizes the asymmetry of time. 'O, call back yesterday, bid time return' laments Salisbury hopelessly in *Richard II*, so that yesterday may stand in for: 'Today, today, unhappy day too late' (*Richard II*, 3.2.65–7). The word *undone* usefully captures this uni-directionality that Shakespeare repeatedly insists upon. 'What's done cannot be undone' reflects Lady Macbeth in her sleepwalking soliloquy (*Macbeth*, 5.1.65). The word *undone* here indicates a vainly hoped-for reversal of something that has been done, and asserts the impossibility of it. But of course the word *undone* could also denote action not taken, something being left undone instead of being done. Most crucially, it could also denote a state of being. This last sense is the most common: Shakespeare overwhelmingly uses *undone* to mean the state of having suffered a calamity that cannot be fixed: '[TUBAL] Antonio almost certainly is undone' (*The Merchant of Venice*, 3.1.11); '[CASSIO] Iago – O, I am spoiled, undone by villains' (*Othello*, 5.1.55); '[NURSE] We are undone, lady, we are undone' (*Romeo and Juliet*, 3.2.38). There are many more such examples.

In order that *undone* should unequivocally denote calamity, Shakespeare takes care always to use the construction *leave undone* when he wishes to invoke the much less common sense of an action that is not performed: '[VENTIDIUS] Better to leave undone than by our deed / Acquire too high a fame' (*Antony and Cleopatra*, 3.1.14); '[FIRST OFFICER] he … leaves nothing undone that may fully discover him their opposite' (*Coriolanus*, 2.2.18–21); '[AUFIDIUS] he hath left undone / That which shall break his neck' (*Coriolanus*, 4.7.25–6); '[IAGO] their best conscience / Is not to leave 't undone, but keep 't unknown' (*Othello*, 3.3.207–8). The only exceptions are where Shakespeare makes a pun on *done* meaning to have sex with, and here still the dominant sense is of an action that cannot be reversed, as in '[KENT] I cannot wish the fault undone' (*King Lear*, 1.1.16) and:

DEMETRIUS
  Villain, what hast thou done?
AARON
  That which thou canst not undo.
CHIRON
  Thou hast undone our mother.
AARON
  Villain, I have done thy mother.
  (*Titus Andronicus*, 4.2.73–6)

In this last example, the symmetrical verbal structure of 'Villain-done / undo-undone / Villain-done' exists precisely in order to stand in contrast to the chronological asymmetry it conveys.

In his use of this *done/undone* phrasing, then, Shakespeare shows his sense of what we now call entropy. Doing is much easier than undoing, or, to take a popular example, one cannot unstir a cup of latte back into its constituents, coffee and milk. If we value a particular state of affairs then it is better to conserve it than destroy it in the hope of restoring it later. A clear practical example is central to the plot of Shakespeare's last sole-authored play, since the ship by which the Italians will leave the island after the end of *The Tempest* is found whole and 'in all her trim' (5.1.239) because it was not split in the first place: its apparent destruction in a storm was an illusion.[10] Those who are said to be undone are very occasionally restored to happiness – as Antonio is in *The Merchant of Venice* – but only because they were not really undone in the first place. Contrary to all reports, Antonio had remaining argosies at sea throughout his apparent calamity, as is revealed at the end of the play (*The Merchant of Venice*, 5.1.287–8). Those who are truly undone always remain undone.

Walter Benjamin's *Theses on the Philosophy of History* contains a reading of a print called 'Angelus Novus' by Paul Klee (created in 1920) that hauntingly captures this idea of the uni-directionality of time arising from the tendency towards chaos:

[The angel's] face is turned towards the past. Where we perceive a chain of events, he sees one single catastrophe which keeps piling wreckage upon wreckage and hurls it in front of his feet. The angel would like to stay, awaken the dead, and make whole what has been smashed. But a storm is blowing from Paradise; it has got caught in his wings with such violence that the angel can no longer close them. This storm irresistibly propels him into the future to which his back is turned, while the pile of debris before him grows skyward. This storm is what we call progress.[11]

Benjamin's sense of a gradually increasing pile of wreckage suits much of the history of our growing technological sophistication, our destructive progress, or as Marxists see it our triumphant negating of the state of Nature. Marxists necessarily agree with the remark of Rose Sayer in the film *The African Queen*: 'Nature, Mr Allnut, is what we are put in this world to rise above.'[12] In Benjamin's account, the wreckage rises skyward, but even this reassuringly suggests that the addition to the pile is just more of the same, just further 'wreckage upon wreckage'. As a Marxist, Benjamin was necessarily aware that sometimes a smooth, linear increase in quantity brings matters to a tipping point where the consequences are no longer linear but exponential; a change in quantity produces a change in quality.[13] We may be well approaching such a tipping point, where more of the same described by Benjamin will produce something truly irreversible.

How this book is structured

Five central questions organize the materials in this book. The first asks how our understanding of the nature of life compares with the understanding shown in Shakespeare's time, when empirical science was just beginning. We have a much better idea than had any previous generation of just what it means for something to be alive, and we can see that the long-standing sharp distinction made between organic and inorganic matter is somewhat artificial. Inorganic matter is as capable as self-replication as is organic matter – computer viruses are a notorious example – and it is also capable of performing logical and arithmetical operations, since of course computers are inorganic. We have for the first time a sense of the interconnectedness of complex global systems – rising ocean temperatures generate violent storms in countries thousands of miles away – yet we have inherited from the history of ideas, which gave us such distinctions as the Renaissance and the Enlightenment, a vocabulary apparently inadequate to the phenomena we must make sense of. As we shall see, some of the ideas of Shakespeare's time are surprisingly useful for seeing beyond the limitations imposed by the terminology of later schools of science and philosophy.

This leads us to the second question: how much attention should we pay to the ideas about the natural world held by people in Shakespeare's time, and evidenced in his works? Seen from one angle, vitalist accounts of Nature appear as outdated as humoral explanations of human biology, or astrological explanations of the cosmos. However, our minds appear to have evolved to take what Daniel Dennett calls 'the intentional stance', in which we attribute motives, goals and states of mind to explain the behaviour of a whole variety of systems, including people, frogs and complex machinery.[14] One of the most obvious examples is a malfunctioning computer, where it makes sense to say, for example, that the printer is 'waiting' for the paper, or that the CPU is 'unaware' that the printer is offline. Thinking in terms of agents and intentions is a heuristic that enables insights unavailable within the narrow bounds of strict materialism. Accounting for the behaviour of frogs only in terms of molecular biology, or the behaviour of computers only in terms of electrical current, does little to help us to understand why they hop, or reboot themselves, in certain circumstances. Viewed in the light of evolution and the intentional stance, early modern accounts of Nature and life appear much more subtle than we used to think.

Our third question concerns how people in Shakespeare's time thought about their relationships with non-human animals, and whether their ideas hold lessons for us now. While certain aspects of early modern Britons' treatment of animals appal us – bear-baiting as entertainment being a signal example – the writings of Shakespeare, among others, suggest the absence of the intellectual prejudices (in particular, speciesism) that later came to dominate thinking about animals and which recent work on animal intelligence, sociability and even what we may call culture renders painfully embarrassing and distasteful.[15]

Fourth, we must ask about the ways that we revise our notions of humanism, religious belief and ethics to accommodate our new understanding of the natural world. The ideas on these topics expressed in Shakespeare's works are frequently offered as models for illustrating the philosophical conflicts that arise in these areas of human belief. Have we been understanding the Shakespearian models correctly?

Fifth, how does the ecological principle of connectedness, as expressed in Barry Commoner's First Law of Ecology – 'Everything is connected to everything else'[16] – help us to compare early modern conceptions of the universe with our own? Unanticipated ecological connectedness has come to light just as late twentieth-century computer technology has given human beings new forms of connectedness in social networks and peer-to-peer communication, including audiovisual media. Accounts of the effect on us of these new ways of being social contain the starkest contradictions of detriment and benefit, from feeding human narcissism and indolence, in endlessly updating a social network profile, to releasing the formerly untapped wisdom of crowds and enabling collective social action planned over secure channels of personal communication. In Shakespeare's depictions, crowds may seem largely fickle, biddable and terrifyingly dangerous, yet early modern theatre crowds seem to have been given extensive powers to censure and change the drama. Tyrannical rulers outnumber beneficent ones in Shakespeare's plays, and oppressed characters voice distinct yearnings for social reorganization that we would identify as a democratic impulse. There are various kinds of collective wisdom manifest in the plays, and some are like the collective forms of wisdom that we are just now learning to draw upon. Are the lessons the same for examples of the reverse position, collective folly, then and now?

All five of these concerns will be addressed across the book's main chapters. The first chapter is about the rise of the new critical school of ecocriticism, and we will survey its core ideas and the historical and literary-theoretical contexts of its emergence since the 1980s. We will consider briefly how ecological and environmental concerns gave rise to this new mode of criticism and how they were moulded into a new interpretative lens through which critics have viewed the works of Shakespeare and others. The relatively small amount of Shakespearian ecocriticism that has been published (all of it post-2006), its various approaches and concerns, will be described and illustrated. The second chapter is concerned with the latest developments in thinking about the relationship between history, biology and culture. It will be argued that ecocriticism needs to be informed by advances in understanding the processes of evolution, which turn out to be rather more complicated than hitherto believed. Evolutionary perspectives provide a model for how ecocriticism may combine recent work in science and philosophy with an historicist concern to understand the past correctly. Here the book will argue for a broadening of ecocriticism's purview to encompass challenging new ideas about the nature of the phenomenon of life itself as an emergent attribute of complex systems.

The third chapter discusses animals in Shakespearian ecocriticism. Some of the clearest markers of the historical difference between us and the early moderns arise from attitudes towards non-human animals. Drawing on Clifford Geertz's essentially literary approach to the practices of unfamiliar cultures – asking 'what did it mean to them?'[17] – Robert Darnton used the Great Cat Massacre of the eighteenth century to illustrate what seemed to him a barely comprehensible change in social attitudes over a period of 250 years.[18] Recent work on early modern attitudes towards animals by Erica Fudge, among others, has presented Shakespearians with an unexpected mix of familiar and alien notions, some of which are strikingly modern in their refusal to make a hard distinction between humans and the other animals. We will consider some case studies of attitudes towards animals in Shakespeare, looking in particular at animals as models for good or bad human behaviour.

The fourth chapter concerns crowds as social networks in their widest sense. The creation of human social networks first made possible by writing, and accelerated, in Shakespeare's time, by movable-type printing, has become the least expected but most culturally significant consequence of cheap information technology. Although circuits of written communication are present in Shakespeare's plays and poems, social groups are most able to behave *as* social groups when they are physically present together, in one place, but early modern theatre had limited resources for representing crowds. Laertes' call to his offstage followers 'stand you all without' (*Hamlet*, 4.5.110) is typical of the sleights-of-hand used to suggest crowds without having to show them.

However, the plays were performed before crowds of as many as 3,000 spectators, who could be co-opted to stand in for the mass audiences (rioters, soldiers, citizens) addressed by their would-be leaders. Shakespeare's few onstage crowds seem all too easily misled – Cinna the Poet is torn to pieces (*Julius Caesar*), and the mindlessly violent Jack Cade is celebrated (*Henry VI, Part Two*); but his crowds can also be restrained and discerning in their judgements. They can become, indeed, more like the social networks enabled by writing. Shakespeare uses animal imagery to characterize onstage and offstage crowds, distinguishing between what we would call distributed organisms (such as ants and bees) and mere swarms of individuals. For genetic reasons, in distributed organisms each ant or bee acts rather like a cell in a multi-cellular organism, so that the colony as a whole is effectively an individual. In swarming behaviour, on the other hand, individuals' actions produce a pseudo-collective form that gives only a temporary illusion of coherent action. Shakespeare explored the motives for different types of collective activity, and his representations of crowds and social networks are cannily insightful about human behaviour. The potential for his insights to help us understand the collective judgements made possible by information technology is discussed in the conclusion to the book.

What emerges from this approach is meant to be both a guide to those unfamiliar with this new critical school, who are hoping to gain a sense of what it offers to Shakespeare criticism, and also an engagement with the discipline that may help extend its boundaries to encompass some of the most pertinent twenty-first-century contexts for reviewing our thoughts on literature. The criticism is avowedly theoretical, but in a way that is intended to contrast sharply with movements from high French Literary Theory from the 1960s, such as structuralism, post-structuralism, deconstruction and postmodernism. These theories may fairly be characterized as self-consolations in the face of the failure of the European revolution of 1968;[19] that is, as theories offering an alternative to political practice. The theory presented here fails to be theory in the sense intended unless it offers readers a means of thinking with Shakespeare, or indeed thinking with any complex literary-historical work, about our present ecological predicament, in order to address the habits of mind and concomitant structures of economic and political power that have given rise to it.

1

The Rise of Ecocriticism

The core thesis of ecocriticism is that our current environmental concerns may provide us with a lens through which to view literature. Whether or not their works are ostensibly about environmental problems, poets and artists necessarily disclose implicit assumptions of their own times, which are often very different from our own and worth considering on that account alone. Moreover, dramatists in particular reflect upon the ways that the fictive human individuals whom they create would, if they existed, think about and respond to the problems thrown up by the socio-political debates occurring in their worlds. In thinking through their characters' responses they often – if they are good artists – tease out the paradoxes and contradictions that make these matters complicated. Shakespeare was writing before the substantial change in shared ideas about humankind's relationship to the natural world known as the Enlightenment. Critics – including me – who believe that certain aspects of Enlightenment thinking have turned out to be mistaken in the light of findings from late twentieth-century science also believe that in certain ways pre-Enlightenment writers such as Shakespeare had a sounder grasp of what was really going on. This was an argument sustained in my book *Green Shakespeare: From Ecopolitics to Ecocriticism*, published in 2006.

Although the Enlightenment cannot safely be reduced to a simple set of principles, the term itself is intentionally reductive in the positive sense of summarizing a complex set of events. By the term Enlightenment we mean to mark a series of contrasts that distinguish seventeenth- and eighteenth-century Western European thinking from what went before it. For our purposes, the three most important of these distinctions are the rise of empirical science as a means to generate knowledge, a powerful faith in the ability of human beings to comprehend and solve problems by the use of Reason and logic (as opposed to superstition, received authority or tradition), and a belief that the rights of individuals are more important than the rights of social classes (especially ruling classes). It is clear that these distinctions suggest a number of corollaries and consequences, including a diminished role for religion and a tendency to link human freedom to democracy. These developments are also noticeably aligned with the needs of nascent capitalism in which contractual relations between individuals replaced older bonds of mutual obligation. We should be wary, then, of simply identifying the Enlightenment with throwing off the chains of medieval thought. Moreover, some of this 'Enlightenment' thinking has roots as far back as the early sixteenth-century Humanism advocated by thinkers such as Thomas More and Erasmus of Rotterdam.

For the purposes of ecocriticism, the most important Enlightenment ideals are the valorization of humankind as a unique category of life – because we are endowed with souls and Reason – and a belief in the inevitability of, and justice in, human mastery of the natural world. These ideas, too, have their origins much earlier than the seventeenth and eighteenth centuries, but this period is nonetheless still usefully labelled the Enlightenment, because almost every intellectual writing in Western Europe was, by then, openly advancing these principles as foundations for further human development. The Enlightenment was an intellectual prerequisite for the Industrial Revolution that followed it, when what we now call economic growth was achieved by the application of new technologies to all forms of production, including (crucially) food production, which sustained population growth. The privileging of human concerns above all others, termed anthropocentrism, is widely understood by ecologists to be an error. Such privileging of the human is speciesist, which is a term, akin to racist or sexist, for the irrational preference for one's own species. Moreover, anthropocentrism is mistaken, because in truth humans form but part of the larger living system that is the Earth considered as a singular self-regulating organism.[1] Anthropocentrism is a characteristic error of Enlightenment thinking.

Because it is concerned with applying the ideas drawn from literary criticism to the present, ecocriticism is inherently a presentist school of thought. The concept of presentism needs some explanation, as it has good and bad senses. Historians have long decried as presentist any writing that anachronistically imports to the study of the past the concerns of the present. Since the nineteenth century, and under the influence of the empiricist historian Leopold von Ranke (1795–1886), who insisted on the centrality of primary sources, historians have striven for an ideal of scholarship that seeks to understand the past in its own terms rather than applying to it the standards, concepts and norms of the present. Holding this as an ideal has not blinded historians to the impossibility of their achieving it: they were and are quite aware that one cannot entirely leave behind one's present-day assumptions and prejudices in order imaginatively to enter the past with no intellectual baggage. The very necessity of attending to one body of evidence rather than another – because rarely can one attend to all the available evidence at once – shapes the narratives that historians write, as Ranke's followers well knew. Indeed, just what counts as evidence can vary from period to period, and evidence is not self-explanatory but rather is constructed by the attention we give to the records available.

In evaluating their source documents from a given moment in the historical past, Rankean historians try to imagine what it was like to be alive at that moment, and ignorant of future events known to the historian. They appreciate that, if they did not try to impose the discipline of such imagined ignorance upon themselves, they might easily read the events of the past as if these were inevitably leading to the present that embodies their completion. For example, in failing to exclude their knowledge, as historians, of the events that followed, they might mistakenly (even unconsciously) impute that knowledge to the historical figures whose actions they were trying to understand. Herbert Butterfield finds an example of this in what he calls *The Whig Interpretation of History* (1931), a nineteenth-century view of British constitutional and social development that celebrated this process' culmination in the Glorious Revolution of 1688.[2] This was presentism in the bad sense.

More recently, however, the term presentism has been reappropriated by those who think the historians' ideal of objectivity through self-imposed ignorance is just a form of self-delusion. Notable Shakespearian publications that have taken this line include Terence Hawkes' book *Shakespeare in the Present*,[3] and the collections of essays called *Presentist Shakespeares*[4] and *Presentism, Gender, and Sexuality in Shakespeare*.[5] According to these critics, we bring to the past so much baggage from the present that objectivity is impossible, and the most honest approach we can take is to be entirely explicit about this and to declare that our interpretations are always utterly shaped by our present-day concerns.

Thus, over the past ten years, presentism has been an approach to literary criticism explicitly evoking present concerns that motivate a desire to review old literature (in particular Shakespeare) to discover resonances that could not have been present for its original audiences or readers because these resonances became possible only as a consequence of what happened between then and now. As such, presentism is a reaction against the dominant mode of historicist analysis that rose to prominence in the two decades after the publication in 1980 of Stephen Greenblatt's *Renaissance Self-fashioning* and the movement called New Historicism that it inaugurated.[6] The objection to New Historicism was that, by concentrating almost exclusively on the past, this once-radical school of criticism was failing to indicate just why old literary texts, such as Shakespeare, were even worth consideration by today's readers. If these texts do not speak to the concerns of the present, what use are they, and why should we even bother to read them?

Carried out properly, historicist criticism itself should bridge the gap between past and present meanings. To treat past meanings as utterly isolated in their own time mistakes the nature of human communication, since if the past was entirely unlike the present then we could make no sense at all of Shakespeare's works. Presentism can usefully be understood as a kind of historicism that shares with Marxist criticism a rejection of the idea that literary meaning is transhistorical, transcultural and embedded in writing from the past; both schools insist upon meaning being generated at the point of consumption by modern readers.

The most vital present socio-political concern for many readers has, in the past ten years, become the environmental crises – including increasingly unpredictable and violent weather and rising sea levels – that are resulting incontrovertibly from the rise in global temperature caused by anthropogenic (that is, human-made) carbon dioxide pollution of the atmosphere. This is not the only socio-political concern of the present, but it is the one that unites the greatest number of the Earth's human inhabitants, and as such it is the prime subject for any presentist study. What follows here is a survey of ecocriticism with particular reference to Shakespeare and to developments since 2006, when the first books on this topic appeared. It is not intended as an exhaustive account of all the work in this field but rather aims to highlight the publications that help reveal where this intellectual discipline has come from, and those that raise particularly important questions about where it ought to be going.

First, some prehistory. The landmark event that recorded the full emergence of a discipline of literary ecocriticism was the appearance in 1996 of a collection of twenty-seven essays comprising a 'reader' on the subject, although (as often happens with such books) many of its contributors traced the origins of the school to earlier and more obscure work. Answering the question 'what is ecocriticism?', the collection's co-editor Cheryll Glotfelty offers a series of definitions, including 'the study of the relationship between literature and the physical environment' based on 'the fundamental premise that human culture is connected to the physical world, affecting it and affected by it', and hence having 'one foot in literature and the other on land'.[7] The examples of interrogations that ecocritics might explore include the alarmingly vague and question-begging 'Are the values expressed in this play consistent with ecological wisdom?'; and the impossibly vast 'How has the concept of wilderness changed over time?'

Across disciplines related to literary studies, ecological awareness began to shape new areas of thought, most recognizably in the 1990s, with specialists identifying earlier ideas relating to current environmental events that were being moulded into a new intellectual lens. In the field of ecolinguistics, for example, the first 'reader' appeared in 2001, and one of its editors, Alwin Fill, provided a useful account of the state of the art that traced how linguists had changed their ideas about the relationship between a language and its environment, with 'environment' understood in a variety of ecological as well as non-ecological senses. Using Critical Discourse Analysis, a number of linguists have traced how writers foreground or efface human agency when writing about various ecological concerns. Alwin Fill highlighted a study by Richard Alexander of an advertisement by the United Kingdom government's Nuclear Industry Radioactive Waste Executive (NIREX) in which agency is expressed in different ways:

2) *Britain* produces nuclear radioactive waste every day …
3) the safe disposal of *our* radioactive waste …
4) some of the most stringent *safety requirements* in the world *will have to be met.*

Agent shift in (2) ('*Britain* produces …') and (3) ('*our* radioactive waste') here implicates everyone in the production of nuclear waste; in (4) agent deletion through passivization ('safety requirements will have to be met') is used as 'a device for distracting attention away from the human actors who have to carry out the disposal process'.[8]

This kind of analysis is recognizably close to literary criticism, differing mainly in its object of attention being an advertisement rather than a literary work.

In *Feminism and the Mastery of Nature*, Val Plumwood addresses the long-standing tradition of associating the natural world with the female gender, and finds it to be a foundational link in the construction of the Western system of knowledge that began in the classical worlds of ancient Greece and Rome.[9] Plumwood's approach is essentially a philosophical one, and she argues that ecological politics will remain hampered by an inability to conceive of environmental crises effectively until the distortions arising from the dominant discourse of masculinist Reason are removed. The problem, according to Plumwood, is dualism, and rather in the manner of a student primer on structuralism she lists the important dichotomies of the Western intellectual tradition, which proceed: 'culture/nature, reason/nature, male/female, mind/body (nature), master/slave'.[10] In each case, the first item in the pair is the dominant one, and it is this that causes these to be harmful dualisms rather than merely useful contrasts: 'In dualistic construction, as in hierarchy, the qualities (actual or supposed), the culture, the values and the areas of life associated with the dualised other are systematically and pervasively constructed and depicted as inferior.'[11] (As we shall see in Chapter 4, there are good reasons to suppose that hierarchies themselves are more properly seen as naturally occurring phenomena than as quintessentially human constructions.)

As a student primer, Plumwood's account stalls at structuralism, failing to mention post-structuralism's much-prized trick of flipping such dichotomies to show that the repressed Other returns to haunt its repressor because, far from being dispensable, it is essential to the definition-by-negation that it makes possible. The deconstructionist's related trick is to show that what look liked naturally occurring contrasts are in fact constructed, and that the mutual interdependency of the two terms – no *culture* without *nature* to distinguish itself from, no *reason* without *madness* – simultaneously binds together and explodes the terms as merely relational and essential linguistics.

Plumwood sees none of this. Indeed, in belabouring the harm of such dualisms, Plumwood's writing approaches unintended self-parody. In her account of 'classical logic', Plumwood remarks on the fact that 'negation ($\sim p$) is interpreted as the universe without p', which definition – she is wrong to call it an interpretation – she finds objectionable because it denies $\sim p$ its status 'as an independent other'.[12] Worse still, according to Plumwood, this negation is a 'phallic drama' in which 'p penetrates a passive, undifferentiated, universal other which is specified as a lack, which offers no resistance, and whose behaviour it controls completely'.[13] In other words, although surprisingly not in Plumwood's words, p rapes $\sim p$. Only after removing such phallocentric power relations from our habits of thought can we grapple with ecology, according to Plumwood. This shallow and distorted account of classical logic did not bode well for the new discipline of ecocriticism.

Shakespearian ecocriticism has an even shorter history than ecocriticism in general. In 2006, Robert N. Watson published *Back to Nature: The Green and the Real in the Late Renaissance*, which also places philosophy at the heart of his ecological approach to literature.[14] Happily, Watson's grasp of philosophical detail far exceeds that of Plumwood. Watson explores how early modern people thought they knew what they knew, the so-called epistemological problem. Watson believes that anxiety about the relationship between reality-in-itself (how things actually are) and perception (how things seem to be) pervaded cultured minds in the late Renaissance, and that a desire to go back to nature expressed a craving for unmediated knowledge, for an originary Edenic certainty.

Watson calls this a yearning – as did Raymond Williams in his classic book *The Country and the City*[15] – but, rather than dispel the sentiment with hard truths of historical materialism, Watson traces its expression in Shakespeare's plays *As You Like It* and *The Merchant of Venice* and other non-Shakespearian poetry and paintings. These cases illustrate a wider phenomenon, for Watson reckons that the anxiety affected not only art but also politics, theology and science.

Watson reads *As You Like It* as though it were called *As You Liken It*, the play being about the inevitability of our settling for likenesses because we fail to grasp things in themselves. In Watson's account, almost everyone everywhere was worrying about the problem of authenticity. Protestant iconoclasts said that no image of God could be accurate, and likewise it was dawning on early moderns, according to Watson, that no image of truth in general can hope to be accurate: knowledge itself is necessarily imperfect. Like Jonathan Bate – who is an ecocritic of writers other than Shakespeare[16] – Watson sees Shakespeare rejecting the subtleties that such philosophical scepticism can lead to, preferring practical and performative goodness over philosophically theorized goodness.[17]

Just because knowledge is necessarily imperfect does not mean that it is utterly different from the thing it tries to know: there are degrees of imperfection that Watson leaves out. Watson might usefully have considered that, because of Charles Darwin's discovery of evolution, we now have sound reasons for supposing that our innate mental tools for modelling reality are in fact pretty accurate, since we inherited them from a long line of successful humans and their pre-human ancestors. From an evolutionary point of view, it is far more simple and efficient for a brain to represent the world as it is than to impose distortions upon the modelling; and by this reasoning a number of philosophical Gordian knots may be cut.

Tracing what happened, historically, after Shakespeare's career had come to an end, Diane Kelsey McColley's *Poetry and Ecology in the Age of Milton and Marvell* is a study of the poetry of the period that argues for its ecological sensitivity at a time when early moderns were just beginning to develop what we think of as the Enlightenment's means for mastering nature.[18] Poets, she argues, could see the coming danger, and 'they both embraced advances in the knowledge of nature and warned against intemperate applications of it'.[19] As might be expected, chapters on somewhat lesser poets lead to a reading of John Milton's masterwork *Paradise Lost*, in which, McColley notices, Eve has a 'strong sense that nature needs' her and Adam and 'that their work is essential to the Garden's well-being'.[20] Moreover, their labour is like the poet's labour in constructing an intricacy. Eve suggests that the climbing plants woodbine and ivy need to be artificially supported – much as the Gardener suggests in Shakespeare's *Richard II* (3.4), although McColley does not mention this – and Milton's verse form matches the image.

According to McColley, 'the thought [of nature's needs] winds from enjambed verse to verse around the pole formed by the beginnings of the lines, as Eve suggests winding the woodbine and the ivy around the trunks of the living trees that form their arbor'.[21] As McColley points out, this is an ethical and political matter, since the words of the winding serpent Satan are not given the same interlacing of content and form: 'the organic connectedness of truth-speaking to natural experience … is the weft on which Milton's paradisal language weaves … [and is] the fabric of ecological consciousness'.[22] McColley finds the same ethics and politics continued in Milton's *Paradise Regained*. Jesus rejects Satan's rationalizations of indulgence in which mastery of Nature is his due by virtue of his humanity – no matter what his divinity entitles him to – and in making this rejection Jesus shows us how to reject 'imperial power, wealth, the authoritarian misuse of spiritual power, [and] the philosophy that elevated human reason above all else', giving us a lesson in 'accepting creaturehood'.[23] Whether or not McColley is right that it is one of the lessons of Milton's poetry, accepting creaturehood is not in itself a useful ethical or political principle for ecological activism, although it might well be part of a helpful dose of human modesty regarding the benefits of progress and civilization.

Ecocriticism that looked squarely and hard at Shakespeare became more prevalent towards the end of the first decade of the twenty-first century. In a collection of essays put together by Thomas Hallock, Ivo Kamps and Karen L. Raber, there is not quite as much Shakespeare as the title, *Early Modern Ecostudies: From the Florentine Codex to Shakespeare*, seems to promise. Georgia Brown's essay naming *Othello* and *Macbeth* is in truth simply about monstrosity and its role in our conceptions of what is normal and natural, and it has little connection with ecocriticism.[24] The only other essay in the collection that engages with Shakespeare is Robert Markley's study of how the Little Ice Age of Shakespeare's time is marked in his works.

An example to which Markley repeatedly turns is the occurrence on six occasions of the stage direction '*storm still*' in the Folio edition of *King Lear*, claiming that its point is not to indicate 'an anomalous weather event' but rather 'a far more familiar experience for Shakespeare and his audiences than it was for his twentieth-century critics'[25] because of the weather's being generally worse at that time due to the Little Ice Age. Sharon O'Dair's and Simon C. Estok's essays name Shakespeare in their titles, but are essentially about Shakespeare criticism as an academic discipline within universities and the various professional contradictions it throws up. Estok manages a little in the way of Shakespeare criticism before getting distracted by the possibility of there being a queer ecocriticism, and digressing into its 'short and unremarkable history'.[26]

Sometimes what sounds promisingly like ecocriticism turns out to be something else. Jeffrey S. Theis' *Writing the Forest in Early Modern England: A Sylvan Pastoral Nation* is highly accomplished literary criticism concerned with writings about forests and trees, including Shakespeare's *As You Like It*, *A Midsummer Night's Dream* and *The Merry Wives of*

Windsor.[27] The omission of the preposition *about* in such phrases as *Writing the Forest* is a post-structuralist tic that has caught on generally as a shorthand way of implying that the writing creates the subject it is concerned with; this once-popular claim is now seldom articulated explicitly, but it lives on in this tic. Theis finds that putting characters into forests enabled Shakespeare to engage with contemporary debates about property rights (the English forests being subject to ancient and frequently incompatible laws and customs) and related debates about the ethics of hunting and poaching. Theis insists, however, that applying what we learn from the plays to present-day debates is unacceptably reductive: 'While Shakespeare's representations of nature usefully speak to our own environmental crisis, his green plots and their relation to early modern forest culture also go beyond this somewhat limited interpretive frame.'[28] This gives us useful parameters for a framework distinguishing what is from what is not ecocriticism: it does not encompass all critical writing about the natural world, since we must exclude criticism that is avowedly non-presentist.

Theis is not alone in wanting to consider Nature and matters green in early modern literature without being labelled an ecocritic. In an early footnote to *The Key of Green: Passion and Perception in Renaissance Culture*, Bruce R. Smith identifies his relationship to 'Nature' as somewhere between that of Timothy Morton, who is sceptical about the word's usefulness, 'and the embrace of the essayists collected in *Green Shakespeare: From Ecopolitics to Ecocriticism*, ed. Gabriel Egan (London: Routledge, 2006)'.[29] (Smith must be mixing up his titles, since *Green Shakespeare* was not a collection of essays but a monograph.)

Downing Cless devotes just one chapter of *Ecology and Environment in European Drama* to Shakespeare, the rest covering plays from the ancient Greek and Roman traditions, Christopher Marlowe's *Doctor Faustus* and writing from the Romantics to the present day.[30] From Shakespeare he selects only *A Midsummer Night's Dream* and *The Tempest,* on the grounds that, although they have elements that appear pastoral (as do other Shakespeare plays), they are in fact conspicuously non-pastoral in presenting a country landscape teeming with interacting natural and supernatural agencies, and in having disruptive weather motivating the dramatic action. For Cless, the cultural upheavals that accompany extreme weather are Shakespeare's primary concern – he shows relationships of love and power being disrupted – and these plays end with culture and Nature harmoniously restored. Thus, 'the nature-within-culture endings of these two plays distinguish them from the utopian versions of Eden in pastoral drama'.[31] This is an important insight, since even if such endings are merely wishful thinking they are not, Cless insists, utopian thinking.

Tying the plays closely to the experiences of Shakespeare as a householder and landowner in Warwickshire, Cless detects a realism about the countryside at the heart of the writing. In this kind of writing, the countryside is not – as it is in pastoralism – merely a place for city-dwellers to recuperate. The plays' wild places are, in fact, niches defined by separateness. The forest does not surround Athens, but is 'a league without the town' (*A Midsummer Night's Dream*, 1.1.165), and the isolated and uninhabited Mediterranean island can be reached only by human maritime technology.[32] These niches are, however, available to all classes: 'Nature in these two plays is not yet a privately owned resource for commodity production, or only a retreat for elites', and according to Cless we can trace this egalitarianism to Shakespeare's 'country roots' and the demotic nature of the open-air amphitheatre playhouses.[33]

In *Ecocriticism and Early Modern English Literature: Green Pastures*, Todd A. Borlik sets out to examine 'classic, as well as a few marginal, works of early modern literature to expose how they document, sanction, or resist' the human capacity to 'explain, admire, and exploit the environment'.[34] Historical works are reread by Borlik looking for their proto-environmentalist feelings, and the literary writers in particular emerge as concerned with problems that concern us now about how humans affect the natural world they rely upon.

For Borlik, the emergence of sixteenth-century Humanism was crucial for its idea of the natural world as a kind of fallen republic that provided a model for egalitarian thinking in which even non-humans might enjoy a right to life rather than existing solely for human exploitation, as Christian readings of The Fall had long tended to assert.

Thus the genre of the pastoral gets from Borlik a rather more generous – less cynical, less ideological – reading than it has in other recent literary criticism, since the pastoral 'invites lay readers to question lifestyles driven by the acquisition of wealth and status, considers issues of environmental justice and land management, and idealizes pre-capitalist economic relations, all the while presenting implicit or explicit critiques of environmental degradation through nostalgic appeals to a (perhaps chimerical) golden age of ecological stability'.[35] As Borlik notes, the infamous destruction of the Bower of Bliss in Edmund Spenser's *The Fairie Queene* is a lesson in moderation – Book 2 is about Temperance – and about limiting one's appetites to natural bounds. Borlik finds that John Milton's masque, *Comus*, pits a burgeoning consumption-led view of Nature against a latent conservative and contemplative one, and sees in both works a reaction to the sudden increase in the burning of coal as a response to deforestation's making timber a newly scarce commodity.[36]

On the same topic was Ken Hiltner's *What Else is Pastoral?: Renaissance Literature and the Environment*,[37] which shows that the continual expansion of early modern London into the surrounding countryside served to highlight what was being lost. To see first-hand the teeming, expanding town of London juxtaposed with the countryside on which it encroached was to perceive forcefully how different they were. The contrast was stark. Hiltner shows that air pollution was a real environmental problem in early modern London and that thinkers were perturbed by it. Hiltner shows that the reactions to environmental destruction became genuine proto-environmentalist movements.

In contrast to Borlik's and Hiltner's sensitive and learned readings of proto-environmentalism in early modern literature is Simon Estok's crude misreadings of Shakespeare, published the same year.[38] Estok wants to bring to ecocriticism his notion of ecophobia meaning 'a pathological aversion toward nature',[39] intended to align the new discipline with other interest-driven critical schools like queer theory (against homophobia) and feminism (against gynophobia). In fact, though, Estok was not the first to use the term ecophobia, as he admits,[40] and in any case the term covers so many phenomena as to be virtually useless. Estok lists possible modern expressions of ecophobia, including: a city sanitation officer's extermination of pests and vermin, the landscaping of gardens, trimmed poodles being kept as pets, and the illnesses of self-starvation and self-harm or 'cutting'.[41]

Viewed through Estok's lens, the image of Shakespeare's achievement is blurred, and his literary criticism holds no surprises for a reader familiar with the plays. Lear 'is a mess, inside and out' (p. 22) and is concerned with space, in that he asks 'where am I?' when he wakes up (p. 29). Lear apparently 'knows Cordelia no better by the end of the play than in the first act; he merely knows his other two daughters better'.[42] Thus Estok makes no concessions to the traditional criticism which suggests that we ought to be touched by Lear's asking for Cordelia's forgiveness when he recognizes that she was right and he was wrong (in Act 1). Estok's chapter on *Coriolanus* concludes that the hero 'clearly needs a different kind of home, a different kind of mother, and a different kind of past', 'is essentially selfish and concerned only with what his people can do for him' and 'is unable to integrate, to show or accept pity, or to offer or listen to speech … [which] spells his undoing'.[43] Such commentary on the plays would attract little credit in an undergraduate essay, and if Shakespearian ecocriticism can do no better the new school deserves to be ignored by readers and playgoers seeking, as a right, criticism that offers insights which they cannot immediately see for themselves.

Fortunately, Shakespearian ecocriticism does exist. As well as Borlik's fine, and Estok's execrable, book, 2011 also saw the journal *Shakespeare Studies* devote a special issue to the topic. Some of the articles share Estok's reluctance to engage in sustained fresh literary criticism and instead reflect, as he did, upon the state of the literary profession. Vin Nardizzi puts the wood used in the construction of open-air amphitheatre playhouses into the context of the late sixteenth-century shortage of timber, noticing that the recycling of the beams of the 1576 Theatre in Shoreditch to make the 1599 Globe would have been sensible even had the Burbage family not been short of the money, which they were.[44] Nardizzi is partly right that when a playhouse put on a green-world play there must have been stimulating analogies between the fictional location and the real site of the performance – stage posts standing in for trees, as they seem to in Shakespeare's *As You Like It*, for example – but undermining this point must be the now well-recognized fact that open-air amphitheatres were so constructed as to disguise their wooden origins.[45] That is, the more they achieved their makers' desire for them to shine like marble, the less apparent would be the parallels that Nardizzi describes.

Uncharacteristically for this collection, Sharon O'Dair's contribution refers directly to a topical ecological disaster: the effects on marine life of the fatal explosion of the Deepwater Horizon well in 2010, which released about 200 million gallons of crude oil into the Gulf of Mexico. Linking a range of responses to the accident with Jaques' famous speech from *As You Like It*, O'Dair asks: 'Do we usurp other creatures even more than we usurp each other, killing "them up / In their assigned and native dwelling place?"'[46] We have seen that ecolinguists and ecocritics share an interest in the ways that word choices and forms of expression can reveal implicit assumptions about an ecological topic. O'Dair identifies the owners of the oil well as the company British Petroleum rather than BP, to which it had changed its name a decade earlier, and amid extensive discussion of the fate of the sea creatures threatened by the spilled oil she omits to mention that the explosion killed eleven men working on the well at the time. As was widely reported, the American president,

Barak Obama, also stressed that the non-American, Old World origins of the oil company were at fault, thereby implying that American oil companies were more diligent. Failing to mention the human toll of the disaster might be seen as taking too far the rejection of human-centred thinking that ecocriticism seeks to encourage.

Ecological concerns are often associated with the colour green because the biomolecule chlorophyll that enables photosynthesis gives plants and algae their green appearance. (Chlorophyll is green, of course, by virtue of being a poor absorber of green light: things have the colour of the light they reflect rather than absorb.) Critics such as Steve Mentz and Dan Brayton think that in ecological studies we overuse the term green, because we concern ourselves too much with life on land, and they want to counterbalance that preoc-cupation by stressing a blue ecocriticism that focuses on the life in the oceans. Mentz explores the possibilities latent in sea and other watery imagery in *Macbeth*, noticing, for example, that the image of 'two spent swimmers that do cling together / And choke their art' (1.2.8–9) is apt because it 'repre-sents impending but not yet arrived disaster' and 'speaks to the dilemma of the Macbeths, torn between their political arts and their desperate desire for human connection'.[47] Moreover, this image of swimmers 'represents green creatures trying, with perhaps only temporary success, to survive in a blue world'.[48]

The obvious objection to this blue turn – here, and in Brayton's book, which attempts to counter the 'terrestrial bias' of ecocritical 'chlorophilia'[49] – is that life-laden seas are in fact green-coloured, because of all the chlorophyll contained in them, and only sea-water that is devoid of life has a trans-lucent blue appearance.[50] What seem to us the beautiful clear blue waters of, for example, parts of the Mediterranean sea are in fact watery deserts devoid of life. Shakespeare was right to think of the ocean as the 'green one' (*Macbeth*, 2.2.61); or at least he was if he was thinking of a healthy ocean full of life.

Evelyn Tribble and John Sutton explore some fruitful connections between ecocriticism and cognitive science, which the present study will also address, because some crucial aspects of the mind arise from its being an evolved organ, and evolution is central to ecological thinking.[51] Cognitive science has recently paid special attention to the fact that we think with the objects around us (that is, our environment) as well as with our minds. Thus, as Tribble shows, we have to understand the early modern playhouses and the routine practices of those who worked in them as providing complex environments that actively aided the actors in their extraordinary achievements of memorizing long scripts, allowing a different play to be performed each day.[52]

An aspect of the ecocriticism/cognition connection, not mentioned by Tribble and Sutton, that makes many literary critics uneasy, is the unavoidable fact that culture changes more quickly than genetic evolution, so that we are thinking with minds that evolved for environments such as the plains of Africa where humans perhaps first emerged, that relatively few humans now live in. This insight is especially disturbing when it is used to suggest that culture is merely a thin veneer that sits atop an essentially uncivilized, ape-like brain, which is how their opponents caricature the fields of sociobiology, evolutionary psychology, and (in some quarters) the entire field of neo-Darwinism when it is used to explain human behaviour. Some effort to confound this caricature will be made in the criticism offered in the present volume.

Also in 2011, the book-form collection of essays called *Ecocritical Shakespeare*, edited by Lynne Bruckner and Dan Brayton, appeared. Among its highlights is a consideration by Rebecca Laroche of what happens if the actor playing Ophelia in *Hamlet* is given exactly the plants she says she is holding and distributing in her mad scene.[53] As Laroche points out, this does not happen in either Franco Zeffirelli's or Kenneth Branagh's film versions of *Hamlet*.[54] Apart from all other considerations, Ophelia seems much less mad if she hands out real plants, rather than twigs or bones; and, as Laroche observes, a practical skill in the art of herbal medicine is just what a young woman of Ophelia's class would have been expected to possess.

Moreover, making an audience consider the possibility that Ophelia attempts to use plants as a restorative as she gradually descends into madness – rather than passing almost instantly into hopeless madness – has the bonus of diverting attention away from Hamlet and on to those whom he callously hurts. Laroche is right to insist that understanding what plants meant to early moderns at that time is crucial to understanding a play that so pointedly invokes their meanings. On the other hand, as Peter Holland points out, it is unlikely that all the plants Ophelia claims to be holding would have been available at any one time of the year, so some element of the imaginary does appear to be invoked by her naming them together.[55]

Being on principle sceptical towards, if not entirely antagonistic to, anthropocentrism, ecocritics are often much concerned with precisely what people, at various times, have believed to be the distinctly human characteristics defining the dividing lines between us and everything else. In *The Indistinct Human*, a collection whose title signals its scepticism on this point, contributors trace to just what extent we are like, or unlike, animals, plants and stones. Indeed, this list provides us with a rough summary of the order of the essays in the collection, so that not until near the end does Jennifer Waldron attend to the various flinty hearts, stony-hearts and stones in the heavens – as Othello calls them (5.2.241–2) – before turning to the living stone of the (supposed) statue of Hermione in *The Winter's Tale*.[56] For Waldron, the key intellectual development was Protestant insistence that mere matter – idols and icons – could not contain divine power or a soul, so that, although Shakespeare's audience could not know whether what looked like a statue was in fact stone or human, they did know that it must be one or the other. Or rather, they could not know until it moved and they discovered that: 'The artifice lay in pretending to be dead stone, not in coming to life.'[57] As Waldron shows, this is something of a reprise of the indistinct death of Desdemona, which is just one in a series of Shakespeare's engagements with the myth of Orpheus, who was able to overcome the resistance of hard physical reality with his art. From an ecocritical point of view, a key lesson here is a reminder that our post-Enlightenment ways of thinking – the distinctions that we make almost by reflex – need to be held in suspension while we investigate pre-Enlightenment ways of thinking and their distinctions.

Bruce Boehrer's *Environment Degradation in Jacobean Drama*[58] ranges across much of the later drama, and shows that there is a distinct theme of the city's spoiling the countryside, and that the writers were conscious that new forms of social interaction were in part to blame for this. The new interpersonal relationships of the city were markedly anonymous and without obligation – no one owes anything unless they have signed a contract – while in the countryside relationships had long been un-anonymous and based on bonds of obligation. This is not merely a restatement of the claim that capitalism replaced feudalism, since, in the opinion of Boehrer, the plays not only reflected this change but also offered playgoers a way to live with it: 'the citizens of Middleton's London were themselves caught in a contradictory situation, forced at once to recognize the loss of an old order of existence and to find ways of living within – and if possible liking – a new one... [His] city comedy offered them a vehicle for doing just this'.[59] The newly gentrified Shakespeare of the early Jacobean years turned away from writing about the healing powers of the countryside to their opposite, which Boehrer calls civil barbarism: 'As a rule, Shakespeare's major Jacobean characters – Lear, Othello, Prospero, Antony, Macbeth, Coriolanus, Timon, etc. – either flee the society of city and court or end up wishing they had.'[60] In general, they do not find comfort but a desolate wilderness.

In *Reading Green in Early Modern England*, Leah Knight considers precisely what the early moderns thought were the physical and biological effects of the colour green, finding that, prior to René Descartes' popularization of a split between the mind and the body, such ideas could take in all the senses, including smell and taste.[61] The writers of lyrics might believe that they had inhaled green-goodness from plants and were now, in the spoken versions of their works, *ex*haling it. Hence, an air was a piece of poetry communicated by wholesome breath, and the sense of smell was thought to be an especially refined faculty, since it is the least corporeal, and the one that takes us closest to the world of spirits. The nose has a hotline to the brain.

Knight explores early moderns' interest in green things, such as trees being capable of emotional responses to well-chosen words, and even of physical movement. In accounts of trees being transported by moving events (including the complaints of humans) we see the entwining of the literal and the poetical, with trees as both object (made to move by powerful poetry or music) and subject (having some volition in what happens). This contrasts rather starkly with the scene in Genesis in which human dominion over Nature is established by Adam's naming its components. Knight sees in the sixteenth-century proliferation of naming schemes – many names for one plant, one name for many plants – the dissolution of this supposed dominion. The supposed dominion retained its power, however, as a model for the poet's dominion over the things he creates.

From this survey it should be apparent that ecocriticism of Shakespeare has some refreshing, novel characteristics as a school of literary analysis. Perhaps the most important is that it trades in relatively straightforward language rather than generating a vocabulary all of its own, as some recent schools have done. The ideas it is concerned with should appeal to a large constituency of readers, especially the young, who will inevitably suffer disproportionately the effects of global warming, as the weather changes and sea levels rise. Ecocritics are in most cases historical scholars whose investigations bring to readers a sense of the way that human beings in early modern Western Europe thought about their relationship to the world, a topic that has an endless capacity to surprise, delight and disturb us.

While certain aspects of early modern Britons' treatment of animals appal us – bear-baiting perhaps most obviously – the writings of Shakespeare, among others, suggest the absence of those anthropocentric assumptions that came to dominate the Enlightenment and that recent scientific studies have invalidated by showing the remarkable intelligence of some animals, with the associated traits of sociability and a transmissible culture. Ecocriticism, ought, then, to be an exciting synthesis of the latest thinking about science and culture, our place in the world, and how the greatest literary artists have reflected upon and represented these things. Done well, that is exactly what Shakespearian ecocriticism is. The following chapters will attempt to illustrate this by example.

My book *Green Shakespeare: From Ecopolitics to Ecocriticism* of 2006[62] is taken out of its historical context in this otherwise chronological survey because its premises largely structure the rest of this book. The most important of these premises is the Gaia hypothesis developed by James Lovelock, in which the entire Earth is considered as essentially a single organism comprising all the component organisms that we generally treat as alive (the biota) together with components of the environment (the Earth's crust, the oceans, the atmosphere) that we have generally believed to be not alive – at least, since the Enlightenment. As I show in *Green Shakespeare*, early moderns did treat the environment as if it were alive: they had a so-called vitalist conception of Nature. But Lovelock's Gaia hypothesis takes us even further than this, since it requires us to accept that the term 'environment' – meaning that which surrounds life – is itself misleading, since the Earth's crust, the oceans and the atmosphere are just as much part of the singular life-form of Earth as are the microorganisms, the plants and the animals that we are accustomed to call life.

Most of what we call a tree is dead matter – there are active cells only in a thin layer under the bark – yet this dead matter is essential to the health of the active cells, which could not live without it: without it there would be no tree. Moreover, the dead matter is not merely a lucky context in which the living parts of the tree happen to exist; rather, the living tree makes the dead part because it needs it. Just as it makes no sense to call ninety-nine per cent of the mass of a tree the 'environment' on which lives the active layer of cells, so it makes no sense to term apparently non-living components of the Earth our 'environment'. Not only are these non-living parts intrinsic to the existence of the living parts, but, moreover, as is the case with the tree, they are actively created in their own interests by the living parts.

Earth's atmosphere being rich in oxygen is not an extraordinary piece of cosmic good fortune simply exploited by the life-forms that use it. Rather, as Lovelock first proved, our oxygen-rich atmosphere was itself created by the life-forms on Earth for their own benefit. This process does not presume planning and a conscious expertise in chemistry on the part of the early life-forms, but rather is one more of the extraordinary benefits of Darwinian evolution. That is, the life-forms that shaped the world to be so hospitable to life are the ones that evolved to do so, their behaviour being rewarded by the same process that, for some of them, rewarded their development of self-locomotive bodies, highly acute eyesight and, finally, self-consciousness.[63] It was in all seriousness that the cognitive scientist and philosopher Daniel Dennett remarked that: 'The planet has finally grown its own nervous system: us.'[64] This compliment entails an obligation upon humankind to use its rare if not unique ability to predict the future and prevent the coming, and foreseeable, environmental disaster.

2

Shakespeare and the Meaning of 'Life' in the Twenty-first Century

Shakespeare was capable of writing extraordinarily beautiful poetry presenting arresting images of natural processes, creatures and settings. Most serious readers and playgoers have their own favourites that stir the heart when they are read or recited. A typical example is this song from one of Shakespeare's late plays:

> MUSICIAN
> (*sings*) Hark, hark, the lark at heaven's gate sings,
> And Phoebus gins arise,
> His steeds to water at those springs
> On chaliced flowers that lies,
> And winking Mary-buds begin to ope their golden eyes;
> With everything that pretty is, my lady sweet, arise:
> Arise, arise!
> (*Cymbeline*, 2.3.19–25)

G. Wilson Knight observes that this play 'is rich in volatile and aerial images, either used by, or associated with, Imogen'.[1] Knight explores this imagery in some detail, from

the references to the puttock and eagle in the first scene
(*Cymbeline*, 1.1.140–1), with the idea of Britain as a swan's
nest (*Cymbeline*, 3.4.140) and of loose Italian women as
jays, to Imogen herself imagined as a dead bird (*Cymbeline*,
4.2.198) and of course the remarkable onstage flight of Jupiter
astride an eagle (*Cymbeline*, 5.5.186). For several pages
Knight pursues this delightful strand of avian imagery of
which the above speech is but one instance.

Yet it is hard not to conclude that Shakespeare deliberately
tempts us to respond emotionally to his beautiful imagery of
the natural world that he found it easy to create only in order
to puncture such a response. Immediately after the above
song, Cloten, who commissioned it as an aubade for Imogen,
says to the singer and his accompanying musicians:

> CLOTEN
> So, get you gone: if this penetrate I will consider your
> music the better: if it do not, it is a vice in her ears, which
> horse-hairs and calves'-guts, nor the voice of unpaved
> eunuch to boot, can never amend.
> (*Cymbeline*, 2.3.19–29)

Horsehairs and calves' guts are the animal body parts that
form the stringed instruments that made the beautiful sounds
to which the aubade was sung. Shakespeare is clearly interested
in just how the sublime is derived from the everyday. 'Is it
not strange,' remarks Benedick, 'that sheep's guts should
hale souls out of men's bodies?' (*Much Ado*, 2.3.58–9).
Self-deflation of his own natural-world sublimities is already
built into Shakespeare's dramatic poetry, a kind of Kantian
immanent critique that explores the material and ideological
bases on which elevated artistic forms are constructed.

It will not do, then, for ecocriticism merely to itemize
Shakespeare's acute sensitivity to the beauties of the natural
world, even when they are as delightful as the imagined
'chaliced flowers' from which the horses who pull the sun-god's
chariot pause to drink the morning's dew. We have already seen

that ecocriticism must be a presentist endeavour, in that it must turn its readings to account in improving our understanding of our early twenty-first-century world, with all the contradictions arising from technologized production and consumption. Moreover, it must be scientific. The Gaia hypothesis is an essential intellectual component in the fight to prevent global warming and other, lesser, ecological disasters. The Gaia hypothesis presents us with the challenge of understanding how something so all-encompassing as a planetary-wide system of self-regulation could have evolved by the processes of biological reproduction as we know them from Darwinism.

This need to incorporate Darwinism means that we must first understand just how inheritance works among individuals, and then how it works among groups living together – including important exceptions to the usual prohibition against the idea of kin selection – and then how individuals in groups work not unlike multi-cellular organisms. This last principle of multi-cellular cooperation is especially important because it allows us to understand why complex organisms (the subject of the third chapter) behave in ways that are similar to crowds (the subject of the fourth chapter). We will find important parallels between inter-cellular communication in biology and the advanced systems of communication that we humans have invented to enable us to behave collectively, as will be explored in the Conclusion, which argues for ecocriticism as a fruitful way of understanding human societies.

In the plays considered in this chapter, Shakespeare performs a series of thought experiments that have two ends. The first is to explore the effects on children of traumas suffered by their mothers in pregnancy and childbirth; the second is to interrogate what we call the Nature/Nurture problem, by separating children from their biological parents and giving them new parents, to discover which is the stronger in influencing their development: biology (Nature), or parenting (Nurture). Shakespeare was alert to the problem that sensitive experiments are susceptible to contamination. For example, in *Cymbeline*, Belarius raises the abducted princes with a strong martial ethic, so that what he understands as their natural sparks of nobility (*Cymbeline*, 3.3.79) might in fact be merely the learned adoption of a positive aspect of courtly ethics – valour and a disdain for gradations of social class – that he brought away from the court with him. The raising of children by adults who are not their parents is a remarkably constant plot element across Shakespeare's plays, reflecting no doubt an early modern reality arising from high mortality rates, especially in childbirth. This becomes a dominant theme in Shakespeare's late plays, but even as early as *A Midsummer Night's Dream* (first performed in 1595) we see a conflict between two would-be foster parents, Titania and Oberon, over who will adopt the orphaned Indian boy.

There is an obvious parallel between, on a personal level, genetic inheritance, and, on a societal level, inheritance of the throne as practised in a monarchy based on primogeniture, as England's was. Solicitous of a smooth monarchical succession in Sicilia, its lords advise their king, Leontes, in the final act of *The Winter's Tale,* to marry in order to produce a new heir. Paulina, however, tells him not to go against the word of the oracle, and offers him the model of Alexander the Great, who: 'Left his [crown] to th' worthiest; so his successor / Was like to be the best' (*The Winter's Tale*, 5.1.48–9). Martin Wiggins recently observed that plays written immediately before the English Civil War are full of switched-at-birth infants, and that this suggests that the best hope that a person dissatisfied with their monarch could hold on to was that he was not their true monarch.[2] In fact, one might reasonably wonder if the point of this plot device was not the rather more politically radical test of just what comprises nobility, and an exploration of whether inheritance by birth is truly the best of all possible forms of government.

Shakespeare's most philosophical play, *Hamlet*, is set in an elective monarchy, and it is sufficiently ambiguous about paternity that the most ambitious recent film production of *Hamlet* suggested by its casting – with the physical likeness of blond-haired actors Kenneth Branagh and Derek Jacobi

– that the prince's biological father was in fact Claudius, and hence that Gertrude's moral failings long predate her hasty remarriage after being widowed.[3] Oddly, for all its subtle exploration of epistemological anxiety, Robert N. Watson's ecocritical study of early modern literature has nothing to say about the uncertainty of paternity.[4]

The only rational understanding of the phenomenon of life available to us in the twenty-first century is Darwinian evolution, which has at its core the theory of how the characteristics of one generation come to be passed on to the next. Shakespeare, too, was deeply interested in the matter of generational inheritance, although of course he lacked Darwin's remarkable insight into slow change. Immediately prior to the widespread acceptance of Darwin's ideas in the late nineteenth century, the dominant model of inheritance was the one offered by Jean-Baptiste de Lamarck (1744–1892). Lamarck's model was evolutionary, in that he saw organisms adapting to their environments and changing their biological structure to better overcome the challenges presented to them. In Lamarckism, cheetahs run faster to catch more gazelles, and descendants of grass seeds blown into dry and stony ground become better at retaining what little moisture they can find. Most importantly, the adaptations made by particular members of a species will be passed on: 'All the acquisitions or losses wrought by nature on individuals, through the influence of the environment in which their race has long been placed, and hence through the influence of the predominant use or permanent disuse of any organ; all these are preserved by reproduction to the new individuals which arise.'[5]

As Richard Dawkins observes, Lamarckism is highly attractive to a certain kind of thinker – his examples were a Marxist historian and the socialist dramatist George Bernard Shaw – because: 'It seemed to offer such positive hopes for the betterment of humanity.'[6] That is, it seems morally agreeable and just that the next generation will inherit something positive arising from the effort that the present generation puts into improving itself. Yet there have also been claims for the positive effect of something precisely the opposite of Lamarckism, the *tabula rasa* theory of John Locke (1632–1704). Locke claimed that the human mind, at least, inherits nothing from previous generations: 'Let us then suppose the Mind to be, as we say, white Paper, void of all Characters, without any Ideas; Whence has it all the materials of Reason and Knowledge? To this I answer, in one word, From *Experience*.'[7]

As Steven Pinker points out, Locke's empiricism seems to offer an attractive biological basis for a principle of egalitarianism underlying social relations. This follows from Locke's belief that:

> differences of opinion arise not because one mind is equipped to grasp the truth and another is defective, but because the two minds have had different histories. Those differences therefore ought to be tolerated rather than suppressed. Locke's notion of a blank slate also undermined a hereditary royalty and aristocracy, whose members could claim no innate wisdom or merit if their minds had started out as blank as everyone else's.[8]

The *tabula rasa* theory of experience-driven knowledge has, since the 1970s, been orthodoxy in Western university departments of the arts, humanities and social sciences. Whatever its attractions for a certain kind of politics, the *blank slate* theory (as Pinker called it) has turned out to be false. That is, we now know that all humans are born with brains highly evolved to behave in particular ways and, consequently, that human nature is real. Pinker provided a list of the universals of human nature that are now empirically demonstrable, from 'abstraction in thought and speech' to 'weather control (attempts to), white (color term)' and 'world view'.[9]

The question of just what each generation inherits from its predecessors and passes on to its successors is sometimes called the Nature/Nurture question. That is, the question can be formulated so as to ask which of those two forces, our inherited capacities or our social experiences, most shapes us. Shakespeare was the first to frame the matter this way, when Prospero called Caliban: 'A devil, a born devil, on whose nature / Nurture can never stick' (*The Tempest*, 4.1.188–9). As we shall see, Shakespeare's last plays insistently explore this question of generational inheritance.

The Nature/Nurture question is crucial because ecocriticism finds its scientific basis in the Gaia hypothesis of James Lovelock, in which the Earth is an evolved system of closely coupled feedback loops that unite organic and inorganic matter into the collective activity we call life. (Individuals whose ecological thinking is not grounded in science have been around much longer than those whose ecological thinking is so grounded, but theirs is a spiritual, even mystical, approach to life, and by definition the rational arguments offered here will not engage them.) It is important to acknowledge, then, that when Lovelock first proposed the Gaia hypothesis it was widely rejected as unscientific. In particular, when proponents of neoDarwinism – that is, the synthesis of Darwin's ideas about natural selection with the genetic model of Gregor Mendel (1822–84), which explained why inherited traits are not blended away – first became aware of the Gaia hypothesis in the 1980s, most thought that it was glaringly guilty of perpetuating the fallacy of group selection that they had spent decades trying to eliminate from popular imagination.

One of the neoDarwinists' greatest challenges was satisfactorily to explain selflessness in individuals. What appears to be altruistic behaviour, such as individuals surrendering their lives for the benefit of others in a group, had long been misunderstood as action for the greater good of the group. NeoDarwinists insisted that genetic selection pressure makes this impossible since, over time, a gene for such suicidal behaviour would necessarily die out with the creatures that expressed it. Since the 1960s, neoDarwinists had been taking the gene's-eye view of such matters and discovered that what looks like altruism from the individual's perspective can in fact be selfishness from the genes' point of view. Because the individuals in a group are often related – sharing the same genes – and because it is immaterial for a gene's survival which individual is carrying that gene, a gene that sacrifices one individual for the sake of helping other individuals who are its relatives carrying the same gene need not die out. The crucial matter is relatedness. Genes that encourage us to help our children or our siblings are genes that encourage us to help copies of themselves. When thinking about the notion of fitness in relation to survival, we have to think beyond the individual carrying the genes that shape behaviour. In our calculation of the effect of a genetic trait on reproductive fitness we have to include – hence 'inclusive fitness' – a count of the copies of the same genes in other individuals. This was first shown mathematically by W. D. Hamilton.[10]

The Gaia hypothesis appeared just when members of the non-scientific public, or at least those who cared enough to look into it, were beginning to understand this gene-centred approach. The Gaia hypothesis appeared to violate the new principles. Dawkins in particular was markedly antipathetic to Lovelock's idea that the entire Earth is a collectively organized system comprising millions of different species. Dawkins' first book, the extraordinary *The Selfish Gene,* that brought the notion of inclusive fitness described above to popular attention, made no mention of Gaia or Lovelock.[11] In his second book, *The Extended Phenotype*, Dawkins went beyond popularizing what was already known about genetic selection in order to develop what he subsequently considered to be his most important contribution to his field: the idea that the structures (phenotypes) built by genes (genotypes) need not be confined to an individual organism's body.[12] That is, we can consider the dams built by beavers to be just as much a part of the phenotypic expression of beavers' genes as are their webbed feet or wood-cutting teeth. By the same token, the worms that parasitize the brains of certain snails and thicken their shells for the worms' benefit (and to the snails' detriment) have in their genotypes the genes for thick shells even though they do not possess those shells themselves.

This brilliant insight into the arbitrariness of our distinctions about where individuals' bodies and agencies begin and end put Dawkins in an ideal position to make sense of the seemingly paradoxical global collaboration on which the Gaia hypothesis is built, but his anxiety to slay the demon of group selection made Dawkins assume genetic naivety on Lovelock's part:

> The fatal flaw in Lovelock's hypothesis would have instantly occurred to him if he had wondered about the level of natural selection process which would be required in order to produce the Earth's supposed adaptations. Homeostatic adaptations in individual bodies evolve because individuals with improved homeostatic apparatus pass on their genes more effectively than individuals with inferior homeostatic apparatuses... For instance, if plants are supposed to make oxygen for the good of the biosphere, imagine a mutant plant which saved itself the costs of oxygen manufacture. Obviously it would outreproduce its more public-spirited colleagues, and genes for public-spiritedness would soon disappear.[13]

Dawkins did not entirely rule out the possibility that a purely neoDarwinian version of Gaia could be modelled, although, he wrote, 'I personally doubt it'.[14]

Lovelock promptly produced the desired neoDarwinian model, DaisyWorld, complete with the requisite cybernetic equations showing how homeostasis, the self-correcting stability that is most characteristic of life, would regulate an entire planet's temperature.[15] Importantly, the regulation was an emergent characteristic of the (admittedly, simplified) planetary system as a whole, not the aim of any particular organism involved in it. That is, by acting strictly selfishly – as neoDarwinists rightly demand – the genes in the daisies modelled by Lovelock's equations collectively produced planetary homeostasis. Since the publication of this proof, Lovelock's Gaia hypothesis has become widely accepted in Earth Systems Science, with the remaining disagreements being essentially terminological.[16] The strongest remaining objection is that Gaia does not show that the entire Earth actually is an organism, but only that it behaves as if it were one. The weakness of this objection is that it begs the question of what it means to be an organism. Most simply put, what is it to be alive?

Ecocriticism after the Enlightenment

Imagine any major European thinker, policy-maker, or opinion-maker living between the years 1700 and 1900 being asked these three questions: (1) Does human activity affect the weather?; (2) Is the Earth alive?; and (3) Are we essentially like other animals? The overwhelming consensus of informed opinion at the time of the Enlightenment and well into the twentieth century would answer no to all three questions, and the questioner's intelligence might, privately, be doubted for asking them. Today, most informed respondents would answer yes to one, two, or all three of these questions. This is a major change in our collective belief system that has been too little considered, and the consequences are significant.

Anthropogenic climate change is widely accepted, especially by those best placed to know, such as professional geographers and meteorologists. Just what would count as the Earth's being alive is tricky to define, but among Earth Systems Scientists there is general acceptance of the main thrust of James Lovelock's Gaia metaphor for the complex chemical exchanges between the world's oceans, atmosphere, and its ever-crumbling rocky crust, forming negative-feedback loops that display self-regulation, a key marker of life. In relation to animals, the turning point is of course Darwin's discovery of evolution and hence the essential continuity between humans and other life-forms. Subsequent zoological work on primates and corvids, in particular, has dispelled the remaining shibboleths: we are not the only creatures to manufacture tools, collaborate on complex projects, teach one another new techniques, use language, or to have a sense of self.

People in Shakespeare's time would have answered yes to all the above questions too, although not for the reasons we do. They had vitalist, astrological and humoral notions that we utterly reject, but the philosophical and political consequences of answering yes to those questions that early moderns faced are the same ones that we face because of them. How should we coordinate our actions to limit the harm we do? Should we conserve the world's resources or use them to transcend Nature for the collective good? How should we treat our fellow creatures? These questions occur across the works of Shakespeare, and the answers that his characters come up with and argue over have lessons for us now. They are questions that were simply ignored for the couple of centuries that we call the Enlightenment.

Epigenetics in Shakespeare

Four of Shakespeare's last plays constitute essentially four thought-experiments that explore the social and personal implications of his society's prevailing ideas about reproduction and inheritance, and they have important consequences for us because key beliefs of his time have turned out to be valid. One of the foundational steps that led to neoDarwinism – which (to restate) is the only sound basis for an ecological understanding of the world – was the germ-line/somatic-line (*Keimplasma/Somatoplasma*) distinction made by August Weismann (1834–1914). By germ-line, Weismann means the sperm and egg cells that exist for the purpose of reproduction, and by somatic-line Weismann means all the other cells that make up the organism's body. The point of this distinction is that the traffic is entirely one-way: the germ-line produces (by reproduction) the somatic-line, but is entirely unaffected by anything that the somatic-line experiences. This Weismann Barrier is the reason that Lamarckian inheritance is impossible. At any rate, that has been the zoological orthodoxy until very recently.

From his earliest plays we can see Shakespeare thinking about what we would call genetic inheritance, and in particular the paradoxes that arise from an organism's creating a descendant that is like itself. For Shakespeare, this offers an explanation for the existence of morality as a consequence of what we would call homeostasis, because bad behaviour is self-punishing. Morality is self-regulation. The earliest example is Lady Anne's curse on Richard Gloucester, in which she imagines him having a child as monstrous as himself:

> LADY ANNE
> If ever he have child, abortive be it,
> Prodigious, and untimely brought to light,
> Whose ugly and unnatural aspect
> May fright the hopeful mother at the view,
> And that be heir to his unhappiness.
> (*Richard III*, 1.2.21–5)

About 160 lines earlier (approximately eight minutes of stage time), Richard had called himself 'deformed, unfinished … half made up' (*Richard III*, 1.1.20–1), so the audience hears Anne cursing Richard with having a child like himself. King Lear pronounces the same curse on his daughter, Goneril:

> LEAR
>   If she must teem,
> Create her child of spleen, that it may live
> And be a thwart disnatured torment to her.
> Let it stamp wrinkles in her brow of youth,
> With cadent tears fret channels in her cheeks,
> Turn all her mother's pains and benefits

To laughter and contempt, that she may feel –
That she may feel
How sharper than a serpent's tooth it is
To have a thankless child.
(*King Lear*, 1.4.273–80)

Having offspring like oneself can be a form of self-punishment:
the parents' wrongdoing rebounds on them when their children
behave in the same selfish way.

It later occurs to Lear that such a rebounding of one's
own wrongdoing might be exactly what is happening to him,
that he is subject to the very curse he made upon Goneril.
That is to say, he wonders whether Goneril might herself be
a deserved punishment to him just as he wishes her child to
be a deserved punishment to her. It is the sight of Edgar that
prompts this horrible thought:

LEAR

Have his daughters brought him to this pass?
Couldst thou save nothing? Wouldst thou give 'em all?

FOOL

Nay, he reserved a blanket, else we had been all
shamed.

LEAR

Now all the plagues that in the pendulous air
Hang fated o'er men's faults fall on thy daughters.

KENT

He hath no daughters, sir.

LEAR

Death, traitor! Nothing could have subdued nature
To such a lowness but his unkind daughters.
Is it the fashion that discarded fathers
Should have thus little mercy on their flesh?
Judicious punishment: 'twas this flesh begot
Those pelican daughters.
(*King Lear*, 3.4.62–74)

Lear comes to realize the errors of his ways, and in this regard we may usefully contrast him with the childless king Richard III. Richard has hopes to start his own line of monarchs, but his imagery of generation runs precisely counter to the principle of transgenerational correction. Richard seems to think that by generation he will undo his crimes rather than be called to account for them:

QUEEN ELIZABETH
    Yet thou didst kill my children.
KING RICHARD
    But in your daughter's womb I bury them,
    Where, in that nest of spicery, they will breed
    Selves of themselves, to your recomfiture.
    (*Richard III*, 4.4.353–6)

The childless Macbeth is like Richard in brutally hacking his way to the throne only to find that it gives little joy without a child to pass it on to. Indeed, we may suppose that these kings are able to be brutal because they are childless: had they to face the transgenerational consequences of passing on these traits they would learn that selfishness is self-defeating.

Thinking about these questions of likeness-in-inheritance, Shakespeare naturally reflected the orthodox belief of his time that what happens to a man and woman during sex, and what happens to the woman during subsequent pregnancy, reach into the womb and affect the baby that is produced. The sex that made Edmund in *King Lear* is discussed by his father in his presence at the start of the play – '[GLOUCESTER] yet was his mother fair, there was good sport at his making' (*King Lear*, 1.1.21–2) – and later by Edmund himself: 'My father compounded with my mother under the dragon's tail' (*King Lear*, 1.2.128–9). Edmund seems to believe that the illicit nature of the sex that made him ('she ... had indeed, sir, a son for her cradle ere she had a husband for her bed' (*King Lear*, 1.1.13–15)), and the very vigour of the act, because it was transgressive, gave strength to his body as he was being created. Thus bastards like him, 'in the lusty stealth of nature take / More composition and fierce quality / Than doth within a dull stale tired bed / Go to the creating ^{Q}of^Q a whole tribe of fops / Got 'tween a sleep and wake' (*King Lear*, 1.2.11–15). (The superscripted '^{Q}...^{Q}' quoted here is the way that the Arden Shakespeare editor R. A. Foakes chose to indicate that the word 'of' appears only in the 1608 quarto edition of the play and not the 1623 First Folio edition; words appearing only in the latter Foakes marked off with '^{F}...^{F}'.)

Edmund's brother Edgar is his very antithesis, and they agree that their differing conditions of creation made for their differences in character and that their father's transgression in making Edmund's is transgenerationally corrected: '[EDGAR] The dark and vicious place where thee he got / Cost him his eyes. [EDMUND] Thou'st spoken ^{F}right, 'tis^F true' (*King Lear*, 5.3.170–1). Throughout Shakespeare we see this idea that what happens in conception and pregnancy shapes the creature that is eventually born. It appears in the story of Jacob's setting parti-coloured wands before Laban's sheep to make them conceive parti-coloured lambs (Genesis, 30.31–40) that is retold by Shylock in *The Merchant of Venice* (1.3.70–89). The Old Shepherd in *The Winter's Tale* even fancies that he can imaginatively reconstruct the venue where the baby Perdita was conceived – 'some stair-work, some trunk-work, some behind-door-work' – and pictures the frantically moving bodies of the parents at that moment: 'They were warmer that got this than the poor thing is here' (*The Winter's Tale*, 3.3.72–4).

In the years since the publication of *Green Shakespeare* in 2006, where I first observed this literary pattern, it has become increasingly apparent that in one particular way the belief of Shakespeare's characters, that the conditions of creation shape the foetus, is in fact true. That is, a foetus really is affected by the experiences of the parents, including those during pregnancy. Confounding all expectation on the subject, the Weismann Barrier has turned out to be permeable so that what affects the somatic-line (the body) may also be imprinted on the germ-line (the sperm and eggs) and future generations inherit effects rising from parental experiences. The most widely researched example concerns women who became pregnant during the Dutch Hunger Winter of 1944–5 caused by a German wartime blockade of Holland's sea-ports.

Epigenesis is the science of gene expression, seeking to explain how particular genes are switched, as it were, on and off. All the cells in an organism other than the sex cells in the testicles and ovaries contain the same doubly encoded genetic sequence. The sex cells, by contrast, have only a single copy that will be combined with the single copy donated by the sexual partner in the act of egg fertilization. The combined maternal and paternal half-shares of genes that together produce the genome of the foetus form a new doubly encoded genetic sequence that will be replicated throughout the newly created individual – except in its own sex cells of course – and this starts with the near-perfect copying of the double code by the repeated cell-division that makes the growing foetus.

This repeated self-division is essentially a process of cloning, and from the initial single cell, the fertilized egg, it produces all the cells needed for the various parts of the human body. The means by which the cells become specialized in the countless different roles they fulfil – as heart muscle cells, skin cells, or brain neurons, and so on – is that for each of these final-destination functions only a part of the full genetic code is used to make proteins within the cell. The other genes, suited to the other final-destination functions that a cell might have ended up fulfilling but did not, are suppressed by the process of epigenesis. The pattern of gene expression is shaped by the conditions in the womb, especially in the first months, which means it is shaped by what happens to the mother during pregnancy.

The Dutch Hunger Winter affected the epigenesis of the foetuses that suffered it, as Nessa Carey explains:

> The cells would change metabolically, in an attempt to keep the foetus growing as healthily as possible despite the

decreased nutrient supply. ... It is probably no surprise that it was the children whose mothers had been malnourished during the very early stages of pregnancy, when developmental programming is at its peak, who went on to be at a higher risk of adult obesity. Their cells had become epigenetically programmed to make the most of limited food supply. This programming remained in place even when the environmental condition that prompted it – famine – was long over.[17]

This contradicts the principle of a Weismann Barrier between the germ-line and the somatic-line, although of course it is not the genotype (the DNA) itself that the experience of hunger altered but the mechanism by which that genotype is, as it were, read in order to create the phenotype (the resulting body). What makes this epigenesis fatal to a strict interpretation of the principle of the Weismann Barrier is that the change can be inherited by the descendants of the altered foetus.

Before this was discovered, cell-to-cell epigenetic inheritance was already known to exist, since it is epigenesis – the control of gene expression by switching genes off and on, or suppressing and unsuppressing them to varying degrees – that keeps cells in their specialist roles. Cells in the top layer of human skin rapidly abrade and are replaced every five weeks by division among the deeper layers of skin stem cells. These fresh clones must inherit the epigenetic programming that controls their gene expression, so that they remain skin cells rather than turning into something else. The revelation was that additional transgenerational epigenetic inheritance exists, even through the male line, where uterine conditions and other alternative explanations are inapplicable.[18]

The plays of Shakespeare's final period, the Romances – *Pericles*, *Cymbeline*, *The Winter's Tale* and *The Tempest* – dramatize how the experiences of a pregnant woman might affect the child she is carrying. Their exploration of how various vectors for transgenerational inheritance – cultural, genetic and epigenetic – make them especially relevant for twenty-first-century ecological rethinking of what it is to be alive, which is the core philosophical problem that the Gaia hypothesis and our impending environmental crises have left us to solve. Thus these plays take ecocriticism beyond the obviously bucolic worlds with which environmentally inflected literary criticism is usually concerned, in order to reflect on the wider global question of the reciprocal relationship between an organism and its surroundings, which is what the Greek origin of the prefix *eco-* (house, dwelling) refers to. Indeed, the revolution in thinking prompted by the Gaia hypothesis perhaps entails an abandonment of our concern for the environment *per se*. If the Earth itself is the collective organism then there is no surrounding region (that is, environment) to speak of.

Creativity and procreativity in *Pericles*

The play sequence starts with *Pericles*, which was first performed in 1607, at about the time that Shakespeare returned to a particular writing practice, collaboration with another dramatist, which he had used for his earliest plays, and that would again, at the end of his career, become his standard practice. About a decade earlier, at the height of his solo-writing career, Shakespeare had produced a remarkable soliloquy on solitary creativity as a kind of self-cloning:

> RICHARD
>   My brain I'll prove the female to my soul,
>   My soul the father, and these two beget
>   A generation of still-breeding thoughts;
>   And these same thoughts people this little world
>   In humours like the people of this world.
>   (*Richard II*, 5.5.6–10)

Imprisoned alone at Pomfret, Richard thinks of his individual creativity as a kind of hermaphroditism in which the mind self-divides to take the male and female roles in creation, which highly fecund ('still-breeding') activity generates yet more creativity. One becomes many. In writing *Pericles*, however, Shakespeare had a fertile artistic relationship with another living creator, his co-author George Wilkins, and perhaps yet another with the dead precursor John Gower, from whom the story was taken – it appears in Gower's *Confessio Amantis* – and whom the play contrived to make live again, as its onstage choric narrator.

Jeffrey Masten has written influentially on the interchange between textual and sexual productivity in this period and in this play in particular.[19] Masten draws on Marjorie Garber's linkage of paternity questions in the plays to the academic anxiety about the paternity of Shakespeare's plays,[20] and comments that even after the recognition of Marina the play 'continues to dwell on … "the undecideability of paternity"'[21] because, Masten believes, the concern is primarily patriarchal: *author* and *authority* are indissolubly linked. Masten traces the chain of certainties about identity back to the document that Pericles put into Thaisa's coffin before it was cast overboard, so that 'his position as patriarchal father, his position of authority – is thus guaranteed only by a text of his own character', and hence in a classic post-structural switch derived from Michel Foucault's author-function, 'The daughter here begets the father; the text begets its author.'[22] Masten explores the parallel with New Bibliographical study of the textual situation, which sought to establish Shakespeare's paternity by casting aspersions of immorality on other agents, including Wilkins and the printers.[23]

The provenance of the play, *Pericles,* is complicated by its being available to us only in the form of a rather garbled edition, a quarto of 1609, that has long been thought to derive from memorial reconstruction. That is, instead of the play's having been printed from an authoritative manuscript descended from the writing of Shakespeare and Wilkins, it is believed to have been printed from an unauthoritative manuscript created by one or more actors from the playing company writing down their recollections of their lines, and those of other characters in the play, and selling the resulting script to a publisher.[24] This memorial reconstruction theory has recently fallen out of popularity as an explanation for textual corruption in general,[25] but it has not been replaced by anything other than uncertainty, and the 1609 quarto of *Pericles* continues to have a problematic authority because of its clear signs of textual corruption.

Questions of textual corruption (which the 1609 quarto shows), and sexual corruption (which the play of *Pericles* is much concerned with), can be interrelated in critical works. Wendy Wall studies the diagrams of lineal descent, called stemmata, that are used by bibliographers to represent the relationships between early texts, and she finds them rather like the lines of familial descent used to represent family trees in the study of genealogy. In both, Wall detects a patriarchal fixation that obscures the complex relationships of text and sex that cut across these lines.[26] In fact Wall is wrong to deride bibliographical stemmata on these grounds, since the relationships between early printed editions of plays really can be thought about in genetic terms. The reason for this is that most commonly a reprint of a play (say, Q2) was made by using an exemplar of the previous edition (say, Q1) as the printer's copy text. Wall is wrong to think that such lines of descent are patrilineal and suppress the matrilineal possibilities, for in fact there really is only one ancestor text (not two) for each descendant. That is, printed editions are made by something like mitosis (cloning) of the parent rather than by meiosis (sexual cell division). Meiosis, sexual reproduction, is a rather better metaphor for the reproductive creativity that happens in authors' minds, as described by Richard II in prison.

Meiosis is what happens when Gower's creativity, fertilized by his sources – 'mine Authors'[27] – including Godfrey of Viterbo (*c.* 1120 to *c.* 1196), was, in the minds of Wilkins and Shakespeare, combined with material from Laurence Twine's *Pattern of Painful Adventures* (1594), which itself took material from the widely circulating collection of stories *Gesta Romanorum* from the late thirteenth and early fourteenth centuries. In the bibliographical stemmata of Shakespeare editions, a single text stands at the head of the monogenetic line of descent, and, by contrast, medieval works are more properly conceived as polygenetic, because the earliest versions are almost always multiple semi-independent manuscripts. In Shakespeare's time, however, Gower's reputation was that of standing alongside Chaucer at the creative head of the entire tradition of English Literature. As Philip Sidney puts it, '[first] wer Gower, and Chawcer, after whom, encoraged & delighted with their excellent foregoing, others haue folowed to bewtify our mother toong'.[28] Of the two, Chaucer's reputation was arguably a little less secure than Gower's, as Ann Thompson shows,[29] but importantly for our purposes Shakespeare only ever acknowledged as his artistic creditors this pair of literary predecessors. Shakespeare's debt to Gower is marked by his appearance in *Pericles,* and his debt to Chaucer by the prologue's notably sexualized reference to him as the work's 'noble breeder' in *The Two Noble Kinsmen* (Prologue, 10).

The recurrence of sexual imagery of artistic fertilization in Shakespeare's collaborative work gives credence to Masten's general claim that collaborative writing excited consciously and unconsciously sexualized descriptions, but it would be a mistake to think that 'the emergent concerns of singular authorship'[30] were simply aligned with heterocentrism. In Shakespeare the contrast is clearly between solitary self-division of the faculties – making the brain female to the soul, in Richard II's soliloquy – by which artistic conception remains monogenetic, and collaboration as a division of labour that in making the work polygenetic risks reducing the dramatist to a mere conduit for another's words and ideas. The abhorrence of incest at the start of *Pericles*, and the dramatization of its avoidance at the end, we can read as necessary self-justifications for a new way of working that Shakespeare adopted in his forties in order to appropriate 'the juice', as Gary Taylor calls it,[31] of younger, more successful men.

Reading (or presumably rereading) the prologue to Gower's

Confessio Amantis in print or in manuscript would have brought certain of Shakespeare's own concerns to the fore. It begins with an acknowledgement that he was writing within a literary tradition ('Of hem that writen ous tofore') and yet creating fresh work ('newe som matiere'), and it names Richard II as the specific catalyst for this particular occasion of creation. The three print editions of *Confessio Amantis*, in 1483, 1532 and 1554, make explicit reference to Richard II, and contain a prologue dedicating the poem to Henry Bolingbroke.[32] This could not fail to bring to Shakespeare's mind his own dramatization of Richard's imprisonment by Henry, quoted above, with its reflections upon the conditions of solitary artistic creation. Reviewing these earlier works, necessarily including his own earlier reflections upon creativity as a kind of sexual act, was Shakespeare's preparatory work for beginning *Pericles* as the first of what we now call his Romances.

In the Romances, sexual reproduction is never straightforward and the offspring are marked by a catastrophe befalling the mother. The first two acts of *Pericles* were written by Wilkins and the last three by Shakespeare,[33] and it is exactly at the point when Shakespeare takes over the writing that the hero's wife, Thaisa, gives birth to her daughter during a storm at sea, for which reason the child is given the name Marina. In his choric narration, Gower reports that Thaisa's fear of the storm itself induced labour: 'The lady shrieks and, well-a-near, / Does fall in travail with her fear' (*Pericles*, 3.0.51–2). Ever conscious of the means of representation by which the story is being told, Gower explains the switch from narration to dramatic performance with 'what ensues. ... Shall for itself itself perform' (*Pericles*, 3.0.53–4). The storm, that is, must be shown with whatever devices the early modern stage can muster, and according to Gower this really is ostension not representation. That is, instead of one thing standing in for another we get the thing itself. Suzanne Gossett suggested that this might be an acknowledgement of the limitations of the stage,[34] but if so it is rather a backhandedly boastful one, rather like the one that the Chorus makes at the start of *Henry V*.

Shakespeare had written scenes depicting storms before this, most notably the storm in *King Lear*, much commented upon by ecocritics.[35] As in *King Lear*, the man on stage opposing himself to the storm apostrophizes it: 'Thou stormest venomously. / Wilt thou spit all thyself?' says Pericles (3.1.7–8). But this is a storm at sea, seen from the point of view of a ship subjected to it, and as with the parallel scene at the start of *The Tempest* Shakespeare thinks of the inadequacy of the aural cues by which the master of a vessel coordinates the actions of his men: 'The seaman's whistle / Is as a whisper in the ears of death, / Unheard' (*Pericles*, 3.1.8–10). Although the 1609 quarto edition of *Pericles* lacks stage directions calling for the sounds of the storm, we may be sure that they were provided in the first performance, else this comment on the drowned-out whistle would make no sense.

The midwife Lychorida enters and hands Pericles his newborn baby daughter and conveys the news that her mother has died in childbirth. Holding the baby, Pericles makes an extended contrast between the trauma of his daughter's entry into the world and the peace that he hopes she will enjoy in life:

PERICLES

                 Now mild may be thy life!
For a more blusterous birth had never babe;
Quiet and gentle thy conditions, for
Thou art the rudeliest welcome to this world
That ever was prince's child. Happy what follows!
Thou hast as chiding a nativity
As fire, air, water, earth, and heaven can make
To herald thee from th' womb.
(*Pericles*, 3.1.27–34)

What follows next in the quarto is Pericles' remark to the baby that 'thy losse is more than can / Thy portage quit with all thou canst find heere'.[36] The Oxford Complete Works editors think that the sense of 'portage' has 'never been satisfactorily explained',[37] but Richard Proudfoot plausibly suggests that this is meant to be a Nature/Nurture contrast. That is, 'portage' covers 'all the endowments that Marina has brought with her' into the world, meaning what she is born with, and this is contrasted with 'all thou canst find heere', meaning what she may make of the world once she is in it.[38]

The next scene introduces Cerimon, who will revive the nearly dead Thaisa. Without any obvious motivation, Shakespeare introduces into this scene Cerimon's own version of the Nature/Nurture binary:

CERIMON
  Virtue and cunning were endowments greater
  Than nobleness and riches. Careless heirs
  May the two latter darken and expend,
  But immortality attends the former.
  (*Pericles*, 3.2.27–30)

Just what Cerimon is contrasting here is somewhat difficult to discern. As a social distinction, 'nobleness' is mainly inherited, although at the time *Pericles* was being written the new king, James I, was creating many new noblemen. For this, King James I was widely mocked, mainly in unpublished writings but also more openly in plays such as *Eastward Ho!* by Ben Jonson, George Chapman and John Marston. Riches can of course be inherited or earned. These 'two latter', nobleness and riches, Cerimon says, may be lost by one's heirs, so clearly his main point is inheritance. Virtue and skilful knowledge – the old meaning of 'cunning' – are, says Cerimon, quite immortal. Since Cerimon cannot be suggesting that virtuous and cunning persons live forever, he must mean that these are legacies that cannot be lost by one's heirs, they are 'endowments' that live on through the generations. Cerimon goes on to explain that 'cunning' is gained by combining study of the 'authorities' – the great writings we inherit from our predecessors – with 'practice' (*Pericles*, 3.2.33–4), meaning experimentation.

Cerimon thus to some degree prefigures the coming breed of empirical scientists of the seventeenth century, and his sense of collective progress arising from empirical work is pure Lamarckism. The Lamarckian route to cheating death – which flatly contradicts the medieval theology dramatized in plays such as the anonymous morality drama *Everyman* – is made concrete in Cerimon's medical skill. He is able to recover only those who are near, not beyond, death (*Pericles*, 3.2.44–5) but believes that reviving the dead is theoretically possible:

CERIMON
    Death may usurp on nature many hours,
    And yet the fire of life kindle again
    The o'erpressed spirits. I have heard of an Egyptian
    That had nine hours lain dead, who was
    By good appliances recovered.
    (*Pericles*, 3.2.81–5)

The early moderns had as much trouble as we have in defining just when a person should be said to be dead. For them, as for us, this declaration is somewhat more of a prediction about the future than a statement about the present. Death is the point beyond which no return to recognizable life is possible, but that can be assessed only by actually attempting to bring the patient back. Hence the heroic measures by which our Emergency Room physicians attempt to restart hearts and preserve brain function, which efforts stop either when they succeed or at an arbitrarily chosen moment when all hope of success has gone. The latter is recorded as the moment of death, although logically this point of no return must have been passed earlier.

The only way to be sure that what has been done cannot be undone is to try to undo it, and Cerimon thinks that the mariners were over-hasty in their decision that all hope was lost: 'They were too rough / That threw her in the sea' (*Pericles*, 3.2.78–9). Although he is renowned for his medical skill, Cerimon does not go as far as Prospero, who claims to have revived the dead (*The Tempest*, 5.1.48–50). Cerimon claims only to have heard that it can be done: 'an Egyptian ... nine hours dead / ... was / By good appliances recovered' (*Pericles*, 3.2.83–5). Successful in his resuscitation, Cerimon uses phrasing – 'Nature awakes; A warmth breathes out of her! She hath not been / Entranced above five hours' (*Pericles*, 3.2.91–3) – that Gossett thought indicative of Cerimon's desire to distance himself from the supernatural power to reverse death itself.[39] The border between life and death certainly has in this play a whiff of magic, as it does in *Romeo and Juliet*, *Much Ado About Nothing*, *Cymbeline* and *The Winter's Tale*; the whiff is supplied here by Cerimon's term 'entranced'. Yet, just as in those plays, the woman who is found to be alive, apparently miraculously, is alive for the mundane reason that, contrary to all appearances, she did not die in the first place. She was not done to death.

We next see Marina as a one-year-old child being left by Pericles with Cleon and Dionyza of Tarsus, whom he asks to provide her with 'princely training / That she may be mannered as she is born' (*Pericles*, 3.3.16–17). Clearly, in Pericles' view of the Nature/Nurture debate, innate nobility of birth will not show through in manners but must be brought out if not entirely created by education. As we shall see, this contrasts with the view of Perdita of most characters in *The Winter's Tale*: Perdita is raised by shepherds but recognized by almost everyone as coming from more refined genetic stock. The pubescent Marina herself seems to feel the epigenetic effect of her birth trauma, although she was of course not conscious of it at the time: 'Ay me, poor maid, / Born in a tempest when my mother died, / This world to me is but a ceaseless storm' (*Pericles*, 4.1.16–18).

For all that Dionyza knows, the murder of Marina that she commissions is obediently carried out by Leonine, although in truth the intended victim was abducted and sold into prostitution by the pirate Valdes and his men. Hence, Dionyza's mocking response to Cleon's disquiet about the deed, 'Why, are you foolish? Can it be undone?' (*Pericles*, 4.3.1), is entirely sincere sarcasm. Murder cannot be undone, for all that Cleon would willingly give the world 'to undo the deed' (*Pericles*, 4.3.6). No Shakespeare play has more occurrences of *undone* and *undo* than the eight that appear in *Pericles* – *All's Well that Ends Well* also has eight – and since seven of them occur in the Shakespearian half (Acts 3–5) this represents by far the highest density of this notion across all his writing. *Pericles* thus forcefully introduces the near-obsession with the hoped-for reversibility of loss that characterizes Shakespeare's Romances.

Dionyza's proposed explanation to Pericles when he comes looking for his daughter is that 'Nurses are not the fates' and 'To foster is not ever to preserve' (*Pericles*, 4.3.14–15). That is, looking after someone's child does not entail giving them any guarantees, and in general life is unpredictable. This is of course sophistry, for what really drove Dionyza to commission Marina's murder was the genetic impulse that drives all creatures to favour carriers of their own genes (as children are) over carriers of others' genes. This unpleasant truth was established empirically by Martin Daly and Margo Wilson,[40] who found that rates of parental assault of step-children are with statistical significance consistently higher than rates of parental assault on biological children, once all other factors (including social class) are controlled for.

In Shakespeare's play, the rivalry between Cleon's and Dionyza's adopted daughter, Marina, and their biological daughter, Philoten, was not hypothetical but, in the mind of Dionyza at least, quite real:

DIONYZA
    She did distain my child, and stood between
    Her and her fortunes. None would look on her,
    But cast their gazes on Marina's face,
    Whilst ours was blurted at, and held a malkin
    Not worth the time of day. It pierced me through,
    And though you call my course unnatural,
    You not your child well loving, yet I find

> It greets me as an enterprise of kindness
> Performed to your sole daughter.
> (*Pericles*, 4.3.31–9)

It would be tempting to dismiss this fear as just Dionyza's imagining and believe that no one really was making such an unfavourable comparison of the two girls. But, as theatre audiences, we hear Gower doing just that: Marina compared to Philoten is a dove to a raven, he says, and in her accomplishments Marina 'darks / In Philoten all graceful marks' (*Pericles*, 4.0.32–6).

At the crucial moment of the encounter between Marina and her future husband Lysimachus, in which he tries to buy her services as a prostitute, she invokes a form of the Nature/Nurture debate applied to the question of whether one's gentility – or nobility or virtue, since the terms are ambiguous and overlapping – comes from one's birth or one's behaviour in life. This particular form of the Nature/Nurture question has a long literary history, figuring, for example, in *The Wife of Bath's Tale* by Geoffrey Chaucer. The old hag at the end of the Wife's story rejects her new husband's dismay at being married to one 'so lough a kynde' (low-born), pointing out that:

> Crist wole we clayme of hym oure gentillesse,
> Nat of oure eldres for hire old richesse.
> For thogh they yeve us al hir heritage,
>
> …
>
> Yet may they nat biquethe for no thyng
> To noon of us hir vertuous lyvyng,
> That made hem gentil men ycalled be.
> (Chaucer, *The Wife of Bath's Tale*, 1117–23)

Marina suggests to Lysimachus a model of gentility that recurs throughout Shakespeare: that it may be inherited or earned, but once granted it places an obligation on the gentleman to behave in a way that is compatible with it. That is to

say, howsoever it is gained, a gentle name may be lost by
behaviour. As Marina puts it:

MARINA
    If you were born to honour, show it now;
    If put upon you, make the judgement good
    That thought you worthy of it.
    (*Pericles*, 4.5.87–9)

Unlike Perdita in *The Winter's Tale*, who is similarly placed in
low surroundings despite a noble birth, Marina knows of her
origins and nonetheless holds behaviour, not noble parentage,
to be the ground of gentleness.

Like Perdita, Marina carries a mind noble in adversity, and
we might think that Shakespeare is rather socially conservative
in suggesting that good birth marks someone indelibly and
that it will show through in later life. In the contrast between
Marina and Perdita, however, we see some rather progressive
thinking from Shakespeare on this point. Not knowing of
her background, Perdita (unlike Marina) suffers considerable
status anxiety about being 'Most goddess-like pranked up'
(as Queen of the Feast) 'in these my borrowed flaunts' (*The
Winter's Tale*, 4.4.10, 23). That is to say, her nurture makes
her insecure despite her noble nature. Conversely, Lysimachus
attributes Marina's goodness to Nurture not Nature, at
least in the 1609 quarto edition: 'thou art a peece of vertue,
& I doubt not but thy training hath bene noble'.[41] For the
Oxford Complete Works edition of the play, Gary Taylor
and MacDonald P. Jackson add a phrase from the prose
novella of the story that Wilkins published the year before
and that they consider to be essentially a report of the play
in performance from which the corrupted play quarto can be
mended.[42] This addition causes Lysimachus in their edition
to attribute Marina's perfection to both Nature and Nurture:
'Thou art a piece of virtue, / The best wrought up that ever
nature made, / And I doubt not thy training hath been noble'
(*Pericles*, 19.137–9).

In this emended version of the text, Lysimachus distinguishes between Marina's inherited physical perfection – 'wrought up' by Nature – and her qualities of personality, that he thinks must have been learned. Shortly after this moment it is indeed her learned, not her innate, abilities – specifically singing, weaving, sewing and dancing – that save Marina, because they turn out to be marketable as skills she may teach. The aristocratic and commercial worlds are not antithetical but complementary, as indeed they were for the entire development of commercial theatre in the late sixteenth century. This theatre industry was stimulated in large part by the mid-century requirement that playing companies find aristocratic patrons.[43] The close proximity of the brothels and playhouses of early modern London, especially on the south bank of the River Thames, would have made Marina's escape from prostitution into a life of rather more refined (yet still commercial) edification seem less implausible than it might to us.

It is impossible to determine whether we are to suppose that Lysimachus went to Marina's brothel looking to buy sex or merely, and innocently, to investigate its sale, as a good governor might if he wanted to prevent the trade in human flesh. In his second meeting with Marina, however, Lysimachus loses audience sympathy by sounding much like Bertram from *All's Well that Ends Well* in regarding difference in social rank to be a barrier to marriage: 'She's such a one that, were I well assured / Came of a gentle kind or noble stock, / I'd wish no better choice and think me rarely wed' (*Pericles*, 5.1.60–2). The parallel is all the stronger, since the task Marina has come to perform is the revival of a sick monarch, as was Helena's in *All's Well that Ends Well*. The scene here, however, is also an unwitting family reunion, so questions of parentage rightly enter into it.

The word *parentage*, which is rare in Shakespeare – occurring nine times across all his other plays – occurs six times in this scene alone. This concern with parentage unifies the play, since (as Gower's epilogue emphasizes) Antiochus and his daughter in the first half represent the worst possible perversion of proper family relations, and Pericles, Thaisa and Marina in the second half the very best. For all their differences in dramatic and poetic skill, Wilkins and Shakespeare must have agreed upon this wider thematic unity to their play as they constructed it. All that remains to spoil the relations of harmony at the close of the play is lingering doubt about Lysimachus. Even if his mission to the brothel was innocent investigation, his proviso that Marina would be acceptable as his wife if her parentage were gentle or noble runs counter to the play's ethos that people should be judged by their actions not their birth. Lingering doubts about the sexual politics of the new grooms and grooms-to-be pervade the endings of Shakespeare's late plays, starting with *All's Well That Ends Well* and continuing with *Pericles*. As Shakespeare developed his Romances into a coherent new genre, the plays' sexual anxieties increasingly coalesced around the uncertainties of paternity.

Genetics and sexual uncertainty in *The Winter's Tale*

The precise chronological order of Shakespeare's plays is unknown, and *Pericles* may have been followed by *Coriolanus*. But his next Romance was either *The Winter's Tale* or *Cymbeline,* and both continued Shakespeare's exploration of the themes that began with *Pericles* of traumatic pregnancy and uncertain parentage. *The Winter's Tale* opens with a visibly pregnant queen, Hermione, whose daughter Perdita is born while her mother is in prison accused of treasonous adultery. Just as Marina is named for the conditions of her birth, so is Perdita. The name is given to her by Antigonus, although he says that the dead Hermione appeared to him in a vision and designated the name because 'the babe / Is counted lost for ever' (*The Winter's Tale*, 3.3.31–2). Since at this point in the action the first-time audience has every reason to suppose that Hermione is dead, this version of events will prevail in their minds.

Once it is revealed, near the end of the play, that Hermione did not die, it becomes apparent that Antigonus cannot have been visited in a dream by her spirit and hence the name Perdita derives entirely from Antigonus' own mind. Antigonus believes that Hermione was guilty of adultery, calling the Bohemian ground where he leaves the baby 'the earth / Of its right father' (*The Winter's Tale*, 3.3.44–5). Thus, as John Pitcher points out, the name Perdita might have been chosen by Antigonus – we would say perhaps unconsciously – because it suggested 'debauched ... morally lost' rather than merely misplaced.[44]

The opening lines of the first court scene gesture quite explicitly to Hermione's visibly pregnant condition: 'POLIXENES Nine changes of the wat'ry star ...', that is nine months, '... hath been / The shepherd's note since we have left our throne / Without a burden' (*The Winter's Tale*, 1.2.1–3). This calendrical reference directly connects Polixenes' arrival in Sicilia with Hermione's being inseminated, and although he cannot mean anything sinister by this – since they are in fact innocent of adultery – the link establishes for the audience an uncertainty about this pregnancy. We know that Hermione is close to labour because of the First Lady's remark to Mamillius that 'The Queen your mother rounds apace' (*The Winter's Tale*, 2.1.17) and because Hermione's delivery, 'something before her time' (*The Winter's Tale*, 2.2.28), happens within a day or two of the opening court scene.

Like Thaisa in *Pericles*, Hermione goes into labour early because of fear: 'On her frights and griefs ... She is, something before her time, delivered' (*The Winter's Tale*, 2.2.26–8). The likeness is shared by their daughters: just as Marina is born to a distressed mother at sea, so Perdita is born to a distressed mother in prison. Indeed, it occurs to Paulina that there is what E. M. W. Tillyard calls a microcosm/macrocosm correspondence[45] at work in a pregnant woman being in jail, since the baby is doubly confined. Nature, of course, works its release: 'This child was prisoner to the womb, and is / By law and process of great nature thence / Freed and enfranchised' (*The Winter's Tale*, 2.2.62–4). The same metaphor of pregnancy as judicial process recurs in Shakespeare's next Romance: 'in the womb he stayed, / Attending nature's law' (*Cymbeline*, 5.5.131–2). So impressed with this image is the Jailer in *The Winter's Tale* that he also frees the baby from the prison he controls, so that Paulina can attempt what Emilia, enthralled with images of parturition, calls a 'free undertaking [that] cannot miss / A thriving issue' (*The Winter's Tale*, 2.2.47–8) in showing the baby to Leontes.

The key question for Leontes is whether the baby is his, and to press her claim that it is Paulina harps upon its likeness to him:

PAULINA

            It is yours,
And might we lay th' old proverb to your charge,
So like you 'tis the worse. Behold, my lords,
Although the print be little, the whole matter
And copy of the father …
   …
And thou good goddess Nature, which hast made it
So like to him that got it, if thou hast
The ordering of the mind too, 'mongst all colours
No yellow in 't, lest she suspect, as he does,
Her children not her husband's.
(*The Winter's Tale*, 2.3.96–108)

Paulina means to show Leontes that he was wrong to suspect that the baby is another's child. But having asserted that the baby is like its father, Paulina must hope that Perdita is unlike her father in one quality at least: that she is not yellow (the colour of jealousy) lest she think that her children are not her own. This is of course absurd, since the uneven burden of sexual reproduction affords women one certainty: they can at least be sure that the children they give birth to are their own.

Even if heritable, Leontes' jealousy could not be transmitted down the female line, as Paulina appears to recognize even as she says this. The Variorum edition of the play cites a number of critics who regard Paulina's absurd thought as intentionally illogical on Paulina's part, as a way to show Leontes his own illogicality.[46] One might argue, however, that what Paulina says is unintentionally inflammatory and that having his attention drawn to the certainty of motherhood Leontes might feel the pain of paternal uncertainty all the more keenly. Either way, Paulina's strategy fails and Leontes does not accept the baby as his. Shakespeare's fascination with daughters separated from their parents, in *Pericles* and *The Winter's Tale*, encompasses not only what they inherit from each of their parents but also how a traumatic birth experience affects the child. That is, he is concerned with what we call epigenetics.

In her trial, Hermione expresses indifference to all worldly concerns, including the preserving of her life, and her absolute concern for what she calls honour, by which she appears to mean reputation: ''Tis a derivative from me to mine, / And only that I stand for' (*The Winter's Tale*, 3.2.43–4). Shakespeare repeatedly dramatized this defiant concern to maintain reputation even at the risk of death, with an early example being Mowbray's: 'The purest treasure mortal times afford / Is spotless reputation; that away, / Men are but gilded loam, or painted clay. … Take honour from me, and my life is done' (*Richard II*, 1.1.177–83). Yet equally often, he dramatized (and rather attractively) his characters mocking these very same ideals of reputation, as with Jaques' image of the soldier: 'Seeking the bubble reputation / Even in the cannon's mouth' (*As You Like It*, 2.7.152–3), or Sir John's 'catechism' against honour as 'a mere scutcheon' (*Henry IV, Part One*, 5.1.129–40). Shakespeare juxtaposed the two views in Iago's mocking response to Cassio's effeminate lament: 'Reputation, reputation, reputation – O, I ha' lost my reputation' (*Othello*, 2.3.256–65).

The constant aspect of these speeches, those in favour of

honour or reputation and those mocking it, is that it is said to be gained or lost by behaviour, not by inheritance. Why, then, does Hermione say that honour is inherited by her daughter ('derivative from me to mine'), whom the king has defamed? Because in this particular case, in which adultery and illegitimacy are alleged, the loss of honour or reputation (by Hermione's alleged behaviour) is inheritable precisely because the alleged offence strikes at the principle of inheritance. That is, just who is designated by the word 'mine' is the issue at stake. This word ought to designate the same children when used by Hermione and Leontes, but that is exactly what the two of them differ on, since Leontes thinks the new baby is not his.

Hermione means to insist that those she calls 'mine' were created honourably (that is, without illicit behaviour) but in saying so she makes the same mistake as the unwitting Paulina: she inflames the situation by drawing attention to the asymmetry of human sexual reproduction that makes maternity certain and paternity uncertain. Hermione can use the word 'mine' with certainty and Leontes cannot. The pronouncement of the oracle from Delphos that clears Hermione uses another possessive pronoun, 'his', in the mirror-image construction to her 'mine': 'Leontes [is] a jealous tyrant, his innocent babe truly begotten' (*The Winter's Tale*, 3.2.133–4). Like Hermione's 'mine', the oracle's 'his' asserts by denotation the very thing it seeks to establish: paternity.

The second half of *The Winter's Tale*, like the second half of *Pericles*, takes place once the girl born in the first half reaches puberty and is sought by sexual partners. Perdita is said – even before the audience has seen her – to look unlike a child born into the family that raised her: '[CAMILLO] ... a daughter of most rare note. The report of her is extended more than can be thought to begin from such a cottage' (*The Winter's Tale*, 4.2.41–3). Polixenes confirms this opinion after meeting Perdita: 'Nothing she does or seems / But smacks of something greater than herself, / Too noble for this place' (*The Winter's Tale*, 4.4.157–9). Unlike Marina, who knows her royal origins, Perdita was a baby when the Old Shepherd took her in and, as we saw, he wrongly guesses her origins. Thus her sense of self is lowly even though others suspect she is high-born. Hence Perdita's discomfort at dressing above her social class, so she thinks, for the sheep-shearing feast, and her further dismay that the prince Florizel, who woos her, has chosen instead to be dressed down as 'a poor humble swain' (*The Winter's Tale*, 4.4.30). In this case, Nurture has given Perdita a false sense of herself that causes her to condemn her dressing up as a kind of artificiality, something Perdita seems strongly to dislike.

Thus, when discussing flowers and their natural and artificial propagation, Perdita expresses a distaste for gillyvors, 'nature's bastards' (*The Winter's Tale*, 4.4.83); we do not know how much Perdita has been told of what the Old Shepherd thinks are her origins, but she shows a sense of distinct shame about them. Emphasizing the analogy she sees between horticultural devices and human artifice, Perdita maintains – in the teeth of Polixenes' justification for their existence – that she will plant no gillyvors: 'No more than, were I painted, I would wish / This youth should say 'twere well, and only therefore / Desire to breed by me' (*The Winter's Tale*, 4.4.101–3). Perdita is obsessed with lines of true descent unsullied by human defilement, and thus she calls Florizel an 'unstained shepherd', as attested by his 'youth / And the true blood which peeps so fairly through 't' (*The Winter's Tale*, 4.4.147–9). Yet she calls him Doricles – which she must know to be a false name, since she knows him to be the king's son – and a shepherd, which are falsehoods. It seems that, although Perdita is anxious about deceit, she draws a sharp line between merely improper pretence (dressing up and using false names) and true moral pollution.

From all this Shakespeare generates the considerable irony of the elevation of the Clown and the Old Shepherd shown in 5.2, since it is by being unrelated to Perdita that they, as it were, inherit a gentle status from her. Were they her biological family, Perdita could not then marry Florizel, and the removal of this impediment saves them. Shakespeare mocks the self-importance of the newly elevated Clown and Old Shepherd, having the Clown utter such Dogberryisms as his assertion that he has been a gentleman born (that is, has an inherited title) 'any time these four hours', and 'I was a gentleman born before my father' (*The Winter's Tale*, 5.2.135–8).

To justify his claim to have been elevated before his father, the Old Shepherd, the Clown describes the scene of reconciliation in terms that sound like a parody of the modern sociological notion of the reconstituted or blended family:

CLOWN
the King's son took me by the hand and called me brother; and then the two kings called my father brother; and then the Prince my brother and the Princess my sister called my father father; and so we wept; and there was the first gentleman-like tears that ever we shed.
(*The Winter's Tale*, 5.2.138–43)

In the English of Shakespeare's time, familial terms that we use quite precisely – *cousin*, *sister*, *brother* – were used more broadly to cover affinities arising from marriage as well as genetic relatedness. In particular, relationships we would qualify with the prefix *step-* are generally not qualified in this way in Shakespeare. Having earlier feared Florizel's plan to make him 'the King's brother-in-law' (*The Winter's Tale*, 4.4.702), the Old Shepherd is now simply his brother.

Although the distinction marked by the suffix *-in-law* is common in Shakespeare, up to this point in his career he had used the prefix *step-* only twice, on both occasions referring to a stepmother or, in his idiom, a 'stepdame'. The first occurrence was Theseus' unpleasant likening of the lingering moon to 'a stepdame or a dowager / Long withering out a young man's revenue' (*A Midsummer Night's Dream*, 1.1.5–6), meaning spending his inheritance by not dying soon enough. The second occurrence was Cressida's use of the antipathy of 'a stepdame to her son' (*Troilus and Cressida*, 3.2.190) as an image of notorious falsehood. The effect of the former use is partially erased by Lysander's expectation of assistance from his 'widow aunt, a dowager' who treats him 'as her only son' (*A Midsummer Night's Dream*, 1.1.157–9), and, importantly, an aunt actually is a blood (that is, genetic) relation whereas a stepmother is not.

Having ended *The Winter's Tale* with this extraordinary image of a reconstituted family in which ties of marriage are treated as if they were as strongly felt as ties of blood – which modern sociological studies have shown to be wishful thinking – Shakespeare then turned to what might be expected to happen next in such a family.

The reconstituted family in *Cymbeline*

In *Cymbeline* the familiar and familial theme of genetic versus social inheritance – the form into which Shakespeare most commonly cast the Nature/Nurture problem – is announced in almost the first speech. What is the matter, the Second Gentleman asks the First? The answer is:

> FIRST GENTLEMAN
> [The king's] daughter, and the heir of 's kingdom, whom
> He purposed to his wife's sole son – a widow
> That late he married – hath referred herself
> Unto a poor but worthy gentleman. She's wedded.
> (*Cymbeline*, 1.1.4–7)

Here the fracturing of the family is on the side of the daughter in the romantic couple, as in *Pericles* and *The Winter's Tale*, but the birth trauma that the play explores is on the side of the son, Posthumus, whose mother 'deceased / As he was born' (*Cymbeline*, 1.1.40). Near the end of the play we learn that Posthumus was born by what we would call Caesarian Section when the ghost of his mother says 'from me was Posthumus ripped' (5.5.139).

Where *The Winter's Tale* puts a princess among fostering farmers, the fostering in *Cymbeline* is done by the male monarch, and his subsequent acquisition of a new wife with a son of her own creates the classic fairy-tale setup of a wicked stepmother scheming against a foster-child (Posthumus), but with the twist that the child is male and rivals the stepmother's biological son for the affections of the princess. The monarch's fostering has been, until recently, careful and lavish, and the recipient is said to have flourished under it:

FIRST GENTLEMAN
   [The king] Breeds him, and makes him of his bedchamber;
   Puts to him all the learnings that his time
   Could make him the receiver of, which he took
   As we do air, fast as 'twas ministered,
   And in 's spring became a harvest; lived in court –
   Which rare it is to do – most praised, most loved;
   A sample to the youngest, to th' more mature
   A glass that feated them, and to the graver
   A child that guided dotards.
   (*Cymbeline*, 1.1.42–50)

Thus far we hear of no consequences of Posthumus' birth trauma, and Cymbeline's recent rejection of him after this generous upbringing reflects all the more unfavourably on the king because of Posthumus' evident virtue. His father in military action against the Romans 'served with glory and admired success' (*Cymbeline*, 1.1.32) and Posthumus himself is one of whom it is said: '[FIRST GENTLEMAN] … to seek through the regions of the earth / For one his like, there would be something failing / In him that should compare. I do not think / So fair an outward and such stuff within / Endows a man but he' (*Cymbeline*, 1.1.19–24).

Shakespeare is not yet finished with setting up his thought-experiment, for in parallel to the son whose mother died in childbirth and who is raised in the court he places the princes who are stolen from the court in infancy and (as we learn when we meet them) are raised rustically:

FIRST GENTLEMAN
He had two sons – if this be worth your hearing,
Mark it: the eld'st of them at three years old,
I' th' swathing clothes the other, from their nursery
Were stol'n, and to this hour no guess in knowledge
Which way they went.
(*Cymbeline*, 1.1.57–61)

The opening scene of the play conveys a great deal of what we now call the back-story, taking as much trouble to set up the complex dramatic situation as the equally densely packed final scene takes to unravel the complications that ensue. For our purposes, the pairing of different childhood traumas – maternal death in parturition and infant abduction – is the key device to hold in mind.

Shakespeare makes no attempt to disguise the fairy-tale aspect of the wicked stepmother motif in the play. Indeed, he has the Queen refer to it in her first lines, as she enters with Imogen and Posthumus, and in a manner that suggests we are overhearing in mid-flow a conversation on the topic: 'No, be assured you shall not find me, daughter, / After the slander of most stepmothers, / Evil-eyed unto you' (*Cymbeline*, 1.1.71–3). The play reruns the exploration of the Nature/Nurture debate in *The Winter's Tale*, in which Polixenes objects to Perdita, because as a farmer's daughter she is too low-born to marry the son of a monarch, but puts it in reverse. This mirror-image of the same situation has Cymbeline object to Posthumus as too low-born to marry the daughter of a monarch, and Imogen fantasizes their equality as farmers' children: 'Would I were / A neatherd's daughter, and my Leonatus / Our neighbour shepherd's son' (*Cymbeline*, 1.1.149–51).

Further complicating *Cymbeline*'s thought-experiment about reconstituted families is a return of the incest motif handled so baldly (albeit by co-author George Wilkins) in

Pericles, and so lightly by Shakespeare in *The Winter's Tale*, in which Leontes is briefly attracted to his long-lost daughter: 'I'd beg your precious mistress' (*The Winter's Tale*, 5.1.222). Posthumus was brought up not merely at court but actually within the household of the king, as Imogen reminds her father: 'You bred him as my playfellow' (*Cymbeline*, 1.1.146). Thus Posthumus is a kind of non-genetic brother to Imogen. Posthumus' rival Cloten really is a brother to Imogen, being a stepbrother, because his mother married the widower Cymbeline, and Cloten uses this word to address her even when he is trying to woo: 'Sister, your sweet hand' (*Cymbeline*, 2.3.84). Yet Cloten is no more nor less biologically related to Imogen than is Posthumus.

Cloten and Posthumus are insistently paralleled and contrasted in the play, being alike as quasi-brothers to Imogen and as rivals for her love. They are distinguished by social class – Cloten's could be no higher, Posthumus' is only middling – and by the regard in which most other characters hold them: Cloten could not be held in lower esteem, Posthumus could not be held in higher. The paralleling and contrasting of Cloten and Posthumus suggests that the roles were doubled by a single actor, which presents no logistical challenges because they never come close to being on stage at the same time. Presented by just one actor's body, all that would visually distinguish the two characters in performance would be their demeanour and clothes, and when Imogen finds the dead Cloten wearing Posthumus' clothes in 4.2 she cannot tell them apart.

In praising Posthumus' clothes – 'His meanest garment ... is dearer / In my respect than all the hairs above thee' (*Cymbeline*, 2.3.130–2) – Imogen meant only to denigrate Cloten's person. Shakespeare spectacularly dramatizes her error so that by wearing Posthumus' clothes Cloten's body inherits all the admiration due to Posthumus' body: 'I know the shape of 's leg; this is his hand, / His foot Mercurial, his Martial thigh, / The brawns of Hercules' (*Cymbeline*, 4.2.311–13). Cloten's earlier reflection that 'the lines of my body are as well drawn as his' (*Cymbeline*, 4.1.9) turns out to be true, and if the roles are doubled we enjoy substantial dramatic irony in Cloten's apostrophizing vow that 'thy head which now is growing upon thy shoulders shall within this hour be off' (*Cymbeline*, 4.1.15–17). Doubling the roles of Posthumus and Cloten has the final additional advantage of making overt the parallel complications regarding sexual attraction within the reconstructed family and the natural family.

That Shakespeare understood how the natural incest taboo worked is clear from what happens when the fractured family of Cymbeline begins to reunite. Imogen's biological brothers are unknown to her, and when they meet there is a distinct incestuous sexual attraction at work:

GUIDERIUS
                              Were you a woman, youth,
    I should woo hard but be your groom in honesty,
    Ay, bid for you as I'd buy.
ARVIRAGUS
                              I'll make't my comfort
    He is a man, I'll love him as my brother.
    (*Cymbeline*, 3.6.66–9)

The taboo against incest is a biological and not a cultural construct, but of course it depends on knowing who one's siblings are. Natural selection operates not upon perfect knowledge of relatedness but by generating rough-and-ready rules that meet most cases, and in human families the rule is to feel revulsion at the thought of having sex with the co-evals one grew up with. This simple rule works most of the time because, usually, one's co-evals are one's siblings. Imogen's brothers did not grow up with her and do not know who she is, so they do not feel this revulsion.

The good report that we have heard of Posthumus at the start of the play is, of course, undermined by his lack of confidence in Imogen, which allows him to be taken in by Iachimo's simple deception. In this he is rather like Othello, although

Iago's skills of deception are vastly more impressive than Iachimo's, and hence Posthumus' gullibility is correspondingly the greater. All the same, both plays invite us to consider just why certain men are vulnerable to sexual insecurity, and gullible, and the ready answer in *Othello* is race. As Hugh Quarshie observes, *The Winter's Tale* shows that Shakespeare was able to create 'a tale about a man coming to terms with the supposed betrayal and adultery of those closest to him without suggesting that a character's race determined his behaviour', so that to make sense of what Shakespeare was up to with Othello we have to understand his gullibility as a racial characteristic.[47] The same logic would require us to understand Posthumus' gullibility by his name and the maternal loss that it denotes.

Convinced of Imogen's infidelity, Posthumus exits from his first meeting with Iachimo in a rage, only to return to the stage immediately to give a soliloquy on female inconstancy that focuses on his mother: 'that most venerable man which I / Did call my father was I know not where / When I was stamped. Some coiner with his tools / Made me a counterfeit; yet my mother seemed / The Dian of that time' (*Cymbeline*, 2.5.3–7). Across Shakespeare's works, one of the commonest pairs of images for procreation is the stamping out of coins and the printing off of sheets of paper. Typical of the former image is Shylock's answer to the question of whether his gold is like livestock: 'I cannot tell. I make it breed as fast' (*The Merchant of Venice*, 1.3.95). Antonio entirely agrees with the suitability of the image, although it revolts him: 'when did friendship take / A breed for barren metal of his friend?' (*The Merchant of Venice*, 1.3.131–2). The latter image recurs in Shakespeare's *Sonnets* when the narrator is enjoining the young man to reproduce: '[Nature] carved thee for her seal, and meant thereby / Thou shouldst print more, not let that copy die' (*Sonnets*, 11.13–14).

The two images of mechanical reproduction, coining and printing, come together when Angelo argues against Isabella's plea for mercy by saying that to permit unauthorized sexual reproduction is tantamount to murder: 'It were as good / To pardon him that hath from nature stolen / A man already made, as to remit / Their saucy sweetness that do coin God's image / In stamps that are forbid' (*Measure for Measure*, 2.4.42–6). The point of this image is to align both kinds of reproduction – of stamped metal, of persons – with recognized authority, and Isabella responds with the appropriate example of unauthorized reproduction, the publishing of books: 'we [women] are soft as our complexions are, / And credulous to false prints' (*Measure for Measure*, 2.4.129–30).

But in sexual reproduction, who is printing whom? Paulina and Leontes implicitly agree that the woman is the mechanism and sexual fidelity is like accurate publication. Of the baby, Perdita, Paulina says: 'Although the print be little, the whole matter / And copy of the father', and, of Florizel, Leontes remarks: 'Your mother was most true to wedlock, Prince, / For she did print your royal father off' (*The Winter's Tale*, 2.3.99–100, 5.1.123–4). Furious with Imogen once Iachimo convinces him of her infidelity, Posthumus is aware that children inherit their natures from both their parents, and hence that part of himself was created by his mother. Although his expression is not completed, he clearly wants to tear out this part much as Romeo wants to tear out his name (*Romeo and Juliet*, 3.3.104–7): '[POSTHUMUS] Could I find out / The woman's part in me – ' (*Cymbeline*, 2.5.19–20).

The association of procreation with coining and printing returns when Posthumus is in jail and, just before falling asleep, soliloquizes an entreaty to the gods: 'For Imogen's dear life take mine, and though / 'Tis not so dear, yet 'tis a life; you coined it' (*Cymbeline*, 5.5.116–17). Giving no credit to his parents as his makers, Posthumus extends his commercial metaphor for creation: ''Tween man and man', meaning in financial transactions, 'they weigh not every stamp'. That is, coins are accepted for their face value not judged by weight. The allusion is to the clipping of coins, the shaving off of gold or silver pieces. In commerce, says Posthumus, such clipped coins are noticed: 'Though light,' merchants 'take pieces

[= such coins] for the figure's sake.' Thinking of himself as such a debased coin, nonetheless carrying the face value of the gods that made him, Posthumus says the gods must accept him: 'You rather mine, being yours' (*Cymbeline*, 5.5.118–20). As Posthumus falls asleep with this image of divine coining on his lips and in his mind, he straight away dreams of, or is visited by (or perhaps both), the ghosts of his mother and father and two brothers.

This ghostly visitation has since the eighteenth century been widely suspected to be a non-Shakespearian interpolation, questioned first by Alexander Pope, who removed it from the text, together with the descent of Jupiter.[48] However, its function within the scene and the wider play is entirely coherent, for it puts on stage for the first time a natural rather than a reconstituted family. This family stands in opposition to Posthumus' mistaken idea that the gods created him, and the members of his family literally oppose themselves to Jupiter in an intercession that reverses Posthumus' fortunes and elicits the written prophecy left by his family upon the sleeping body of Posthumus. The prophecy uses images of natural procreation and organic growth – 'a lion's whelp ... a stately cedar ... lopped branches ... jointed to the old stock' (*Cymbeline*, 5.5.232–6) – to represent the denouement's replacement of reconstituted families with natural ones. For all that it takes a supernatural intervention to create it, *Cymbeline* ends with familial harmony that is matched by wider social and geopolitical harmony, taking the form of a British peace treaty with Rome that occurs at just the historical moment when God's only son Jesus Christ is born. The play, then, insists upon the primacy of natural families.

The material that Pope excised from the play included an innovation in staging – the flying of Jupiter – made possible by his playing company's acquisition in August 1608 of a theatre, the Blackfriars, that undoubtedly had a machine by which an actor could be lowered to the stage from the room above it. We know that the Blackfriars had a descent machine because one is needed for the stage direction '*Hymen* descends' in

George Chapman's play *The Widow's Tears*, performed by the boys' company there in 1604–5.[49] None of Shakespeare's deities descends from above before Jupiter does in *Cymbeline*, which suggests that the Globe playhouse did not originally have a descent machine. Retro-fitting a descent machine to the Globe would have made sense once the Blackfriars was acquired and the practices at the two houses regularized so that both used act-intervals and both put their musicians into the stage balcony.[50] In his last sole-authored play, *The Tempest*, Shakespeare repeated this use of a theophany-by-descent as a supernatural intervention, and as in *Cymbeline* he pitted inherited against learned goodness in a further exploration of the power of Nature versus Nurture.

Learned and innate virtue in *The Tempest*

Setting up the Nature/Nurture binary for his final thought-experiment in *The Tempest*, Shakespeare used a joke that remains effective in performance. Attempting to explain to his daughter, Miranda, her surprising origins, Prospero says: 'Thy father was the Duke of Milan', to which she responds, 'Sir, are not you my father?' (*The Tempest*, 1.2.54–5). This, Prospero jocundly chooses to take as if it impugned his wife: 'Thy mother was a piece of virtue, and / She said thou wast my daughter' (*The Tempest*, 1.2.56–7). The same suggestion of maternal infidelity resurfaces, only to be dismissed, as soon as Miranda hears the story of the theft by Prospero's brother Antonio of the dukedom of Milan: '[MIRANDA] I should sin / To think but nobly of my grandmother. / Good wombs have borne bad sons' (*The Tempest*, 1.2.118–20). By saying this, Miranda is immediately established as rather more sophisticated in relation to inheritance than the one-dimensional Belarius in *Cymbeline*, who simply concludes: 'Cowards father cowards, and base things sire base' (*Cymbeline*, 4.2.26).

Optimism about inheritance follows from Miranda's sentiment, since if bad people can come from good wombs then presumably the reverse can also happen. Thus it became Miranda's project to educate Caliban. The origins of Prospero's earthy servant are laid out in the form of a rebuke of his airy servant, who has complained of his servitude:

PROSPERO
    This blue-eyed hag [Sycorax] was hither brought with child
    … the son that she did litter here,
    A freckled whelp, hag-born – not honoured with
    A human shape.
ARIEL
                Yes, Caliban her son.
(*The Tempest*, 1.2.270–85)

Prospero's diction of 'litter' and 'whelp' is consistent with his claim that Caliban is not human, but Ariel confirms the story by calling him her 'son', which sounds rather like an implicit demurral on that point. Sycorax was banished from Algiers for what Prospero claims were 'mischiefs manifold and sorceries terrible / To enter human hearing' (*The Tempest*, 1.2.265–6), meaning that they are unspeakable. Yet, 'For one thing she did / They would not take her life' (*The Tempest*, 1.2.267–8), which might either be some good that Sycorax did the people of Algiers or might be her pregnancy itself, which was grounds for the commuting of a death sentence in Shakespeare's England.[51] The assumption that pregnant women are spared execution underlies Joan of Arc's failed attempt to convince her British captors that she is pregnant, in *Henry VI, Part One* (5.6.62).

While Sycorax was still carrying the foetal Caliban she was punished with banishment by the Algerians and sent to the island now ruled by Prospero. Within a few lines of revealing this, Prospero adds detail to his version of Caliban's story, calling him a 'poisonous slave, got by the devil himself / Upon thy wicked dam' (*The Tempest*, 1.2.321–2). If literally true this makes a considerable difference to our understanding of the significance of the play, but we cannot know if it is true because Prospero's only source of information – Ariel having no apparent skills of divination – is Caliban himself, who can know only what his mother has told him. This is intentional uncertainty on Shakespeare's part, reinforced by the play's recurrent expressions of uncertainty expressed about Caliban's nature. He is called a monster by those who would control him, but is human enough for Miranda to consider him a man when musing to herself: 'This [Ferdinand] / Is the third man that e'er I saw' (*The Tempest*, 1.2.447–8), her father being the first and Caliban the second.

Shakespeare's habitual association of sexual reproduction with printing recurs when Caliban remembers with pleasure his attempted rape of Miranda and its wished-for outcome: he could have 'peopled ... / This isle with Calibans' (*The Tempest*, 1.2.352–3). His intended victim rebukes him with language that is notably strong for a young Jacobean noblewoman – '[MIRANDA] Abhorrèd slave' – but she immediately moderates this with a cogent explanation of her disdain for him: 'Which any print of goodness wilt not take' (*The Tempest*, 1.2.353–4). That is, Miranda considers Caliban incapable of moral improvement from his innate state of evil. This is not to say that he could not be educated, but, as Miranda and Prospero discover, the learning of language is not the same as the acquisition of either goodness or civilization.

Self-evidently, Caliban was able to learn English. Miranda distinguishes between what can be learned and what is innate: 'thy vile race, / Though thou didst learn, had that in't which good natures / Could not abide to be with' (*The Tempest*, 1.2.360–2). Miranda appears to take the pessimists' side in the long-running debate about whether virtue is learned or innate, which Plato in his dialogues *Protagoras* and *Meno* divides into two distinct questions: whether virtue can be taught, which if true would require someone to be its teacher; and whether it can be learned, for which life's experiences may suffice as the teacher. Famously, of course, by the end of this play Caliban appears to have learned virtue from his experiences as a follower of Trinculo and Stephano, and instigator of their abortive rebellion.

The main plot of the play is a parallel attempt by Prospero to teach a lesson in virtue to his usurping brother Antonio and his accomplices, and it is not unambiguously a success. Antonio is given no lines to speak to Prospero in the final scene by which he might apologize or even acknowledge his wrongdoing. Prospero's forgiveness of Antonio emphasizes both their relatedness and what seems to be a resigned acceptance that his brother has not changed:

PROSPERO

                    Flesh and blood,
    You, brother mine, that entertained ambition,
    Expelled remorse and nature ...
                    ... I do forgive thee,
    Unnatural though thou art.
    (*The Tempest*, 5.1.74–9)

Although the usurpation of Prospero is technically reversed by the restoration of his rights, the ruptured family is not healed as it was in *Cymbeline*.

The closest that the final scene comes to a statement of general harmonious resolution comes from Gonzalo: 'in one voyage / Did Claribel her husband find at Tunis, / And Ferdinand her brother found a wife / Where he himself was lost; Prospero his dukedom / In a poor isle' (*The Tempest*, 5.1.211–15). In an earlier access of anarchism Gonzalo had imagined himself experimenting on this poor isle with the development of a society without hierarchies, in which unfettered nature itself should 'bring forth / Of it own kind all foison, all abundance' (*The Tempest*, 2.1.168–95). As Sebastian and Antonio mockingly commented at the time, the corollary of such a state of Nature is the absence of the social institution of marriage that regulates sexuality: 'No marrying

... [all] whores and knaves' (*The Tempest*, 2.1.171–2). At the close, with the island's glorious visions of possibility faded, the best Gonzalo can do is to restate the consolations of marriages and restored rights, the very triumph of the cultural over the natural that he had earlier wished away.

Gonzalo's attempt to construct imaginatively an ideal commonwealth is not mere hubris but reflects a widespread impulse to perfect human society that derives from admirable human fellow-feeling. If ecocriticism has to resist anthropocentrism, does it not then tend towards the kind of misanthropy, expressed by Sebastian and Antonio, that can find no value in such fellow-feeling? If human nature is essentially a genetic matter then what in any case is the point of trying to perfect human society at all, since we cannot change the fundamental nature of people? With no chinks in the Weismann Barrier to allow experience to alter genetics, there might seem a plausible logic to such counsels of despair.

NeoDarwinists have, of course, long pointed out that even evolutionary psychologists and sociobiologists do not argue that our genes utterly determine who we are: they acknowledge the place for human culture in our behaviour. The new discoveries in the field of epigenetics might soften the opponents of evolutionary accounts of human nature and enable them to consider the politically progressive aspects of the field's insights. While it ought not to be the deciding factor in such matters, it is gratifying to a certain progressive political mind-set to learn that there is in fact a chink in the Weismann Barrier and that Locke was not entirely mistaken about our experiences writing themselves upon us.

Coda: Printing, procreation and the market for writing

Somebody involved in the creation of the 1623 First Folio of Shakespeare evidently thought that Belarius had made a profound statement with his rhyming couplet: 'Cowards father cowards, and base things sire base. / Nature hath meal and bran, contempt and grace' (*Cymbeline*, 4.2.26–7). These two lines are picked out by preceding quotation marks in the Folio text, which was the convention for what is called commonplacing: the marking of *sententiae* that a reader might wish to extract from a text and keep as nuggets of portable wisdom.[52] Yet these lines do not strike us as especially wise and it is hard to believe that Shakespeare marked them off to highlight his poetic or philosophical achievement. Presumably someone else involved in the transmission of the play thought that this couplet was worth the repeating.

We know for certain that someone in the print shop recognized another part of *Cymbeline* as being undoubtedly repeatable, because of its actually being repeated in the play. This is the prophecy given to Posthumus. The prophecy is spoken by Posthumus when he awakes to find it lying on his breast (*Cymbeline*, 5.5.204–38), and again in the final scene when the Soothsayer explains how its terms have now been fulfilled (*Cymbeline*, 5.6.436–53). The compositor setting the type for this prophecy noticed that it was read verbatim twice and he saved himself the trouble of setting it twice by putting aside the block of type containing it in scene 5.5,[53] rather than distributing its type back into his type case, and then he inserted this saved block whole for the second reading in 5.6.[54] To use Shakespeare's own metaphor of printing being like procreation, this is perfect inheritance, perfect copying, perfect iterability. It stands for what the printing press could do in the way of perfecting the reproduction of words.

Shakespeare was right to see analogies between printing, sex and genetic transmission of likeness, as a number of critics have shown.[55] The printing press made possible textual reproduction that was intellectually fecund just as sexual reproduction is biologically fecund. Manuscript writing, and even older technologies, had long preserved human thoughts beyond the decease of their thinkers. But printing revolutionized thought, because multiple copies of a piece of writing enabled thinkers across the known world to be in contact with one another. By such a social network, thinkers could keep up with the collective progress of thoughts that built one upon another – this happened first in the European Reformation of religion and then again in the development of science – and allowed them even to anticipate the intellectual questions that other thinkers might be working on in order that progress could be collectively advanced.

Even as Shakespeare was writing *Cymbeline* in 1609–10, his exact contemporary Galileo Galilei (1564–1642) was watching the skies with his new optical instrument, the telescope, and discovering that the geocentric model of the universe propounded by the Greco-Egyptian astronomer Ptolemy (*c.* 90–168 CE) was incompatible with his obser-vations and that something like the heliocentric model of Nicolaus Copernicus (1473–1543) must be right. Galileo published his *Sidereus Nuncius* (= *Starry Messenger*) early in 1610 in order to be in time for the Frankfurt Book Fair, the printed catalogue for which circulated among the intellectuals of Europe.[56] This catalogue, more than the Book Fair itself, created a social network of thinkers who knew – at least insofar as they could infer it from book titles – what other members of the group were working on.

The Winter's Tale, *Cymbeline* and *The Tempest* were not printed until the 1623 Folio collection appeared, and the book was given advance publicity by inclusion in the 1622 catalogue of the Frankfurt Book Fair.[57] *Pericles* appeared in 1609 in a badly mangled text that cannot reflect how Shakespeare wished it to be read. Lukas Erne has established that Shakespeare wanted to be a successful author in print (as well as a writer for the stage) but also that he achieved that ambition.[58] A curious part of the story of this achievement is that, after an extremely successful run of sixteen first editions in the 1590s and early 1600s, the period from the publication of *Hamlet* in 1603 to Shakespeare's death thirteen years later saw the publication of just two more first editions – *King*

Lear in 1608 and *Troilus and Cressida* in 1609 – plus the bad quarto of *Pericles* in 1609.

It is not clear why the first editions dried up, but unless Shakespeare was himself planning what became the 1623 Folio – which is not impossible[59] – then in the second half of the 1610s he would have been quite rightly anxious about his print legacy. From the late 1590s, his play editions began to blazon their paternity on their title-pages, but shortly thereafter came the drought of first editions that imperilled his intellectual legacy. It was at this point that Shakespeare began a series of plays about what and how the next generation inherits from the present one. It is not unreasonable to suppose that, as Shakespeare approached his half century on Earth, he began to give considerable thought to legacy and inheritance in their biological, creative and intellectual forms. His last plays dramatize extreme disruptions to family life that are, finally, overcome but not, as in his comedies, by the complete triumph of joy and harmony. Rather, the late Shakespeare plays entail seemingly intolerable losses – of Mamillius, of Antigonus, and others – that nevertheless have to be borne. Loss, they seem to say, cannot be undone, but it can be ameliorated, tolerated and lived with. As ecocriticism enters its own maturity, that in itself is an important lesson.

3

Animals in Shakespearian Ecocriticism

Almost all human beings have cells containing the genes from two parents in a random 50/50 per cent mixture: half from the mother and half from the father. A few people, however, have genetic material from three people because as foetuses they were created by a procedure known as cytoplasmic transfer. Ordinarily, an egg contains two sets of genetic material: that of the cell itself and that of the cell's mitochondria, which are specialized subunits within the cell, responsible for specialised tasks, including the production of chemical energy. Unlike the main DNA of the egg cell, the mitochondria's DNA is not combined with the DNA from the sperm cell but, rather, passes down the female line unchanged except by mutation over time. So, in the natural way, a foetus will receive the mother's mitochondrial DNA unchanged in its own mitochondria, while its cell DNA is a combination of the DNA of the two parents. In cytoplasmic transfer the mitochondrial DNA is donated by a third party, typically to overcome genetic defects in the mother's mitochondrial DNA.

In February 2015, the United Kingdom government authorized the medical procedure of cytoplasmic transfer – leading to so-called 'three-parent' babies – and many commentators rightly remarked that such parenthood entails a fundamental change in our notions of how biology underpins the social structure of the family. No commentators remarked that the fact that almost all Earth's creatures have an independent genome within each cell, the mitochondrial DNA, that is inherited down the female line is an extraordinary consequence of the origins of the earliest complex life-forms. The matter is not settled to the satisfaction of all biologists, but the prevailing explanation – the work of James Lovelock's collaborator, Lynn Margulis – is endosymbiotic theory, and it suggests that we have biological collaboration to thank for the existence of all complex multi-cellular life. According to this theory, for much of the early history of life on Earth there were only single-cell organisms, prokaryotes, which had no mitochondria and no complex internal mechanisms that might enable the development of sophisticated life-forms. At some point, colonies of quite different prokaryotes formed symbiotic unions – possibly by one ingesting the other without destroying it – that turned out to be highly profitable to both.[1]

If this is the case, life as we know it arose from mutually beneficial collaboration, not destructive competition. When animals collaborate for mutual benefit – and humans are the best at such collaboration – they may be repeating the process that gave rise to them. In the next chapter we will consider the ways in which collaborations between cells within individuals resemble the various forms of collaboration between individuals at higher levels of social organization. Between these levels of interest exist some fascinating creatures – in the main social insects – for which it is truly difficult to say just where the individual organism starts and finishes. Does an entire ant or bee colony constitute an individual or is it composed of individuals working together? This is an important question for ecocritics, since the Gaia hypothesis requires the existence of a worldwide biological interconnectedness that runs counter to how we have hitherto thought of life. Before we discuss this topic, however, we must examine how animals were understood, and theorized about, in Shakespeare's time. If ecocritics are to overcome the dominant ideology of anthropocentrism, a new account of animals' place in the world is required.

*

Historians of the early modern period have for the most part studied other animals in order to understand how human beings have conceived of their place in the universe, to see 'the ways in which humans define themselves as human in the face of the animal'.[2] As Erica Fudge's work has shown, the effort to construct a clear ontological boundary between animals and humans has, at least since the early modern period, repeatedly failed. As post-structuralist theory predicts, the binary opposition between animals and humans relies on a negation – the quality of being not-human – that undermines itself, since this is a relationship of reliance upon the opposite, the Other, for self-definition.

Moving to concrete examples, Fudge examines accounts of animal-baiting in the bear-houses of Shakespeare's London[3] and finds numerous examples of what we may call boundary confusion. An ostensible function of such public animal shows was to enable even the lowest-born human spectator to experience pride in being demonstrably superior to at least some living creature. Yet, despite the appeal of their (apparent) demonstration of human distinctiveness – monkeys and bears behaving like humans but clearly not being humans – these entertainments were recurrently described by thoughtful commentators as being as disturbing as they were delightful, not least for reducing the spectators to the level of beasts and dignifying almost to sanctity their animal victims.

René Descartes famously asserts in *Discourse on the Method* (1637) that non-human animals are essentially machines because they lack the self-awareness arising from possession of the rational soul that makes humans uniquely special. This stark conclusion strikes us as absurd, but Fudge usefully situates it in the context of a world in which machines were becoming increasingly impressive. More importantly, the realities of economic activities – colonial expansion, increased urbanization and expanding technological powers of production – fed an urgent need to justify human domination of all creation.[4] We can, if we wish, give these developments a more positive construction and conclude that Descartes gives a rational basis to the principle, first propounded by Jesus Christ but consistently acted on by his followers, that all human beings are equally deserving of special consideration solely by virtue of being human.

Descartes firmly established a sharp and easily articulated and understood distinction between humans and animals. As Bruce Boehrer shows, there was a loose consensus on this topic a few decades earlier, in Shakespeare's time, but it was far from clearly defined and without problems.[5] The Great Chain of Being model (detailed below) that placed humankind above the animals and below the angels allowed for various kinds of metaphorical and allegorical expression of approval and disapproval of human behaviour. Thus a brave soldier might be imaged as a 'lion's whelp', but cowards likened to 'the weasel' that 'Comes sneaking' (*Henry V*, 1.2.109, 170, 171). The trouble is, as Boehrer points out, that the coherence of any such simplified system of categorization will be threatened by the anomalies of the very cases it may be used to decry: 'How does one account for the elements of creation that do not conform to the particular modes of binary organization one has already chosen as significant?'.[6] In short, is such a system modelling the world as it is, or merely as we would like it to be?

Prior to Descartes, Boehrer shows, the human characteristic most commonly asserted to distinguish us from animals was Reason, expressed in the faculty, seen as unique to humans, of language. For us, now, in the early years of the twenty-first century, of course, this criterion has become of diminished utility, since we are increasingly discovering hitherto unsuspected abilities among our fellow, non-human, animals to reason and use language. In a later book, Boehrer traces a series of case studies of early modern thinking about human relationships with a range of creatures – horses, parrots, cats, turkeys and sheep – to see what light these might throw on how we come to think of ourselves when we find animals displaying attributes we thought distinctively human.[7] For Boehrer, the processes of classification by distinction-making that informed thinking about human–animal relations in the seventeenth century formed the basis for wider generic distinction-making within literary culture in the eighteenth and nineteenth centuries. Baldly put, we have animals to thank for the emergence of English Literature. For example, the novel's obsession with human interiority puts into literary practice the Cartesian philosophy of human uniqueness.

Although acknowledging her debt to Fudge and Boehrer, Laurie Shannon argues that focusing too much on what earlier writing about attitudes towards animals can tell us about attitudes to being human – animals being 'good to think with' – has the demerit of drawing attention away from the historical fact that early moderns thought of animals 'as actors and stakeholders endowed by their creator with certain subjective interests'.[8] Far from being mere property to be used instrumentally, animals were accorded what we might loosely call rights. Moreover, it was widely noted that animals had not fallen with Adam and Eve, and were naturally provided with all that they needed for existence, while humans come into the world lacking the bare necessities. Animals, by comparison, are happy in both senses of that word: fortunate and contented.[9]

These studies of early modern ideas about animals tell us much about what people thought in Shakespeare's time, and how thinking about animals helped them to think about other things, including the best ordering of human affairs. These studies are especially welcome for redressing what is starting to look like a glaring and embarrassing myopia regarding animals in our anthropocentric tradition of English literary criticism. These studies do not, however, tell us just how far we really are like other animals, how much we really have in common with them. Since the animals themselves have shown no sign of wanting to do that either we need human studies of biology for that, and, as ever, the genetically informed approach is essential. What it tells us is that some early modern ideas that were dismissed out of hand during the anthropocentric period of the Enlightenment are in fact quite correct.

The dominant way of thinking about the ordering of the universe in Shakespeare's time was a model described by E. M. W. Tillyard as the Great Chain of Being.[10] In this model, each kind of object in the universe is allocated a place in a hierarchy, from the lowest kinds of object (rocks and other inanimate matter), through the lower and higher forms of terrestrial life, up to the higher beings and finally to God. Rather than seeing the living and non-living entities of the universe as arranged in strictly divided classes with little in common, the Great Chain of Being draws on Aristotle's idea that 'after lifeless things in the upward scale comes the plant, and of plants one will differ from another as to its amount of apparent vitality … there is observed in plants a continuous scale of ascent towards the animal'.[11] This idea of a continuous scale of differences between entities, as opposed to discrete classes of entities, arises from Plato's account of the creation of the world in *Timeaus*.[12]

A core Christian principle seems incompatible with Aristotle's and Plato's idea of a superabundant world teeming with minutely variant species arranged in a hierarchy. For Christians, humankind is supposed to be the whole point of the universe, not just one rung on a ladder of creation. Arthur O. Lovejoy examines how medieval theologians dealt with this,[13] and in Tillyard's view the early modern reconciliation of Christianity with inherited classical and pagan ideas was an imperfect compromise between Christian and Classical, true, of course, of much Renaissance thinking.

The metaphor of a chain used to represent ranking order is especially appropriate because it implies tension in the model. Each element of the universe is linked to the one above and below by this chain, and within each category there is thus a pull in two directions. The link to a higher group exerts an upward pull on an entity and the link to a lower group exerts a downward pull. Take the lion. The very best quality of such a 'high' animal reaches almost the status of the worst aspect of humanity, while its worst quality is like that of a 'lower' animal. This allows for a metaphor of primacy: as the lion is the king of beasts, noble in being so much better than the other beasts, so a king who excels among kings may be called lion-hearted, like Richard I (1157–99), known as Coeur-de-lion. A lesser monarch, like the Duke of Austria, may enter 'wearing a lion's hide' (*King John*, 2.1.0) to give himself something of that quality, only to be mocked by another, Constance: 'Doff it, for shame, / And hang a calf's-skin on those recreant limbs' (*King John*, 3.1.55). In this case, the bastard son of Richard the Lionheart picks up the mocking cry and makes it a refrain (*King John*, 3.1.57, 59, 125), indicating that if Austria is like any animal it is the ignoble cow, not the lion.

This kind of implicit metaphorization is easily missed if one is not sensitized to it by Tillyard's account of the Great Chain of Being. In an early work of proto-ecocriticism, Jeanne Addison Roberts argues that Shakespeare's plays at first dealt with this animal–human metaphorization in a comic mode – employing the 'secure hierarchy of the Great Chain of Being' – but that he began to see the connection as more literal than metaphoric. By the end of his career, Shakespeare was making genuinely hybrid characters, such as the part-fish-part-man-puppy-headed monster Caliban, in a recognition that 'the chain may be horizontal rather than vertical ... narrowing [the] gap between man and animal'.[14]

Tillyard drew attention to the inclusion in the Elizabethan World Picture of a principle of correspondence between the planes of existence, the various cosmic scales ranging from the individual body to the family unit, the human society and other collections of creatures, and up to the heavenly bodies. There are, according to the Picture, useful analogies between the principles applying at each level: the head rules the body as a father rules his family as a king rules his people as the Sun rules the heavens, and so on.

To this way of thinking, our social structures might have parallels with those of other animals:

MARCUS
    Alas, my lord, I have but killed a fly.
TITUS
    'But'? How if that fly had a father, brother?
    How would he hang his slender gilded wings
    And buzz lamenting dirges in the air!
    Poor harmless fly,
    That with his pretty buzzing melody
    Came here to make us merry – and thou hast killed him!
    (*Titus Andronicus*, 3.2.59–65)

A fly has family connections and its own concerns just as we have: it is part of the Chain of Being. This moment might well be comic, but it has a serious implication. To us a fly may seem unimportant, but to another fly it might be a family member, a loved one, and indeed these other flies might grieve for its loss. Ordinarily, we do not notice their family relations because we do not live among the flies. We now know that Titus is mistaken – flies do not live in families – but the first audiences did not know this and the challenge to our assumptions of alienness stands: how do we know they are not like us?

Humankind was also, until Shakespeare's time, largely thought to be physically located at the cosmological centre of things. Within Shakespeare's lifetime, there were beginning to emerge good reasons to question the validity of this belief. Since ancient times it had been believed, in the West at least, that the Earth was at the central point of a physical universe comprising heavenly bodies that revolved around it. Astronomers Nicolaus Copernicus (1473–1543) and Galileo Galilei (1564–1642) challenged the prevailing view and argued that the Sun was at the centre, orbited by the Earth. (We now know that this, too, is wrong: the Sun is an insignificant star among many billions of stars.) Throughout Shakespeare's career, Copernicus' view was known, but it was not widely accepted until Galileo, in 1610, proved, by showing its moon-like phases, that Venus orbits the Sun. According to Tillyard, 'the ordinary educated Elizabethan' was aware of Copernicus' ideas but rejected them, or at least their inherent implications.[15] We might say the same for current attitudes towards anthropogenic climate change: grudgingly accepted but not lived as a truth.

The standard history-of-ideas interpretation of the seventeenth- and eighteenth-century Age of Enlightenment is that all the early modern commonplace ideas described by Tillyard went the way of the geocentric model. Using rational and empirical investigation, the physical and zoological theories of the early modern period were, in the Enlightenment period, replaced by newer and more accurate ideas. The denigration of animals that this entailed – which led to the view of Descartes and his followers that we have nothing in common with animals – was part of this process, but in the light of the work of Fudge and others it is hard not to see this so-called Enlightenment itself as a sort of collective wish-fulfilment. That is, animals were asserted to be unlike us because it became increasingly intolerable to think that we and they might be essentially the same.

Recently, science has given us reason to ponder whether there are aspects of the Elizabethan World Picture useful for conceptualizing the complexity of life on Earth, especially the preponderance of macrocosm/microcosm correspondences and the arbitrary distinctions we make between living and non-living matter. There are newly discovered macrocosmic/microcosmic correspondences that puzzle the mind, including fractals and holograms.[16] Self-similarity is what the Tillyardian Picture exhibits, and if early moderns believed in it then they were on to something. The most important self-similar system of all (as far as we know) is the Earth itself – if, as most Earth systems scientists believe (to a greater or lesser extent), the Gaia hypothesis of James Lovelock is fundamentally true.

Transposed into the chronological axis, a Great Chain of Being in which creatures vary one from another by tiny differences is precisely what Darwinian evolution forces us to accept. Indeed, Darwinism itself raises what is called the species problem apparent in the Great Chain of Being. How can we say that the giraffe belongs in a category distinct from its neighbours if creatures are separated by only slight individual variations? Darwin himself tried and failed to explain why evolution has produced creatures that appear to fall into discrete, non-overlapping categories; and in the light of his ideas it might be argued that the concept of discrete species is only a product of the tendency of our minds towards categorization.[17] The current consensus is that this is mistaken and that the term 'species' is a valid taxonomical distinction, and yet the problem of how evolution produces clear gaps between species, rather than producing hybrids combining two closely related species, is not yet resolved.[18] Explanations based on how the geographical isolation of populations leads, over time, to distinct groups that cannot interbreed – which seems a useful way of thinking about what characterizes distinct species – raise their own, additional, problems when natural populations decline and the majority of the individuals concerned live in zoos.[19]

'Forgiveness, horse!'

Horses were essential to the economy and social life of early modern England, as traction power and as a means of personal transport.[20] Together with dogs and cats, they were the animals most commonly encountered by early moderns without thought of eating them. Horses feature prominently in the stories told in early modern plays, but apparently for practical reasons they were seldom if ever represented on the stage. In an inventory dated 10 March 1598 listing the properties of the playing company called the Lord Admiral's

Men, the theatre impresario Philip Henslowe recorded 'j great horse with his leagues'.[21] W. W. Greg speculated that this was the wooden horse of the Greeks to be used in a play about the siege of Troy, which would explain its greatness and that the legs were apparently detachable. There is no other record in Henslowe of a property horse, which we would expect to find if it were usual to depict with onstage properties the horses frequently referred to in the plays of Shakespeare's time.

The apparent avoidance of the direct depiction of horses in the drama is especially marked in Shakespeare's *Richard II*, a play that seems to set the audience up to expect a representation of trial-by-combat on horseback only to deny them that pleasure. The trial arises from Richard's failure in the opening scene to effect a reconciliation between Henry Bolingbroke, heir to the dukedom of Lancaster (held by his father John of Gaunt), and his enemy Thomas Mowbray, Duke of Norfolk. Richard decrees that 'swords and lances [will] arbitrate' their accusations against one other (*Richard II*, 1.1.200). In early modern combat, it was possible for swords and lances to be wielded by combatants on foot as well as on horseback[22] but the audience expects that the encounter will be on horseback in this case because in the second scene the Duchess of Gloucester hopes that 'Mowbray's sins [sit] so heavy in his bosom / That they may break his foaming courser's back / And throw the rider headlong in the lists' (*Richard II*, 1.2.50–2). An audience used to the normal form of trial by combat with lances will expect the depiction of horses, yet there is nothing in 1.3, the trial scene, that suggests the presence either of real or property horses.

Shakespeare seems here to repeatedly raise and deflate expectations. His dialogue says that the trial will be on horseback, but the stage shows no animals. The combatants get close to commencing their trial, but Richard interrupts it to frustrate them – and indeed the onstage and theatre audiences. The trial occurs because Richard could find no way to enforce forgiveness between Bolingbroke and Mowbray in the opening scene. Forgiveness is a key theme of the play, the word recurring in the mouth of the Duke of York when he counsels the new king Henry IV that to forgive his, York's, son Aumerle (newly renamed Rutland) would serve only to incite the forgiven and his accomplices to further treachery (*Richard II*, 5.3.81–4). In the event, York's son is forgiven. The word forgiveness occurs for a third and final time in Richard's scene in prison, when surprisingly it is asked of a horse.

In the prison scene, a former groom of Richard's stable describes how, at the recent coronation of Henry IV, the new king rode upon Richard's favourite horse, who seemed proud of his burden. Hearing this, Richard rails at the animal for not exacting revenge by throwing off its rider, thus echoing the Duchess of Gloucester's prayer for Mowbray's horse to throw him off. On reflection, Richard regrets this railing as unfair: horses are bred to be proud of their riders, and so: 'Forgiveness, horse!' (5.5.90), he says. Musing further on his state – a habit developed during his extended isolation in prison – Richard imagines himself as such an animal, mistreated by its rider: '[I am] Spur-galled and tired by jauncing Bolingbroke' (5.5.94). To jaunce can mean to make a horse prance, or indeed to prance like a horse oneself, so jaunty Bolingbroke – the adjective has the same origin – is here to be imagined riding Richard and making them jaunce together, to the rider's delight and his mount's humiliation.

Only one other play of the period seems to require the onstage representation of a horse, and it tells the same story as Shakespeare's. Indeed, Samuel Rowley's *Thomas of Woodstock* not only tells the same story; it also draws heavily on Shakespeare's *Richard II* for its language.[23] In 3.2 of *Thomas of Woodstock* appears the stage direction '*Enter a spruce courtier a horsebacke*' and the ensuing dialogue indicates that the animal is walked about the stage.[24] W. J. Lawrence thought this play the one indisputable example of a live horse appearing on the early modern stage, making it 'a remarkable exception to the general rule' that they did not.[25] If so, it was a remarkable theatrical occasion not only for the spectacle of a real horse on the stage but also because of how the horse is treated.

As he walks the horse about, Woodstock talks gently and sympathetically to the animal, remarking that 'you haue sweat hard about this hast' and noticing the animal's underfed and overworked condition. By contrast, the rider is 'spruce', meaning well-kempt, and yet the horse has 'as much witt' as its rider. As a response to Shakespeare's *Richard II*, the scene touchingly realizes the sympathies latent in Shakespeare's prison scene between Richard and the groom. Woodstock's affectionate 'youle followe any man that will lead you' echoes Richard's realization that to blame the animal for its inbred servility is to mistake its nature.

The horse at least does not mistake appearance for substance. Woodstock is given the task of walking the animal to cool it down after its day's riding because the 'spruce courtier' had mistaken Woodstock's plainness of clothing – he does not dress like a duke – and assumed that he had encountered merely a groom of the household rather than its head. Thus the spruce courtier left his abused horse with the duke while he went into the house to find the duke. Rowley, like Shakespeare, could imagine his characters seeing beyond the usefulness of a horse as a source of power and locomotion to perceive a sentient being deserving of kindness.

Andreas Höfele argues that when early modern writings address the human/animal distinction they most often see not a pair of separate categories but rather one folded within the other.[26] That is, humans contain their animal and vegetative origins. This turns out to be a rather keen insight into the biological reality of human nature, as well as into our ideas about ourselves. Since human beings gradually evolved from organisms with less sophisticated brains than we have, it would not be surprising if some of what we call thinking had its origins in internal messaging systems rather less complicated than our systems of neurons, synapses and axons. Antonio R. Damasio has pointed out that this is precisely what has happened: our cognitive systems based on electro-chemical signalling are built to work in tandem with simpler and slower systems of internal signalling by hormones carried in the bloodstream.[27] To a certain extent, then, we think with our emotions, and rationality cannot be separated from somatic feeling. As Daniel C. Dennett points out in a review of Damasio's book, this means that 'a self distributed throughout the body' is 'a clear descendant of the Aristotelian vegetative soul'.[28] Ecocritics are necessarily alert to such occasions, when the latest scientific thinking takes a detour around high Enlightenment thinking about the human condition to alight on something rather more subtle that preceded it.

'Hounds and greyhounds, mongrels, spaniels, curs'

Caroline Spurgeon famously argues that Shakespeare had a decidedly low opinion of dogs.[29] She notes that Shakespeare was particularly concerned with dogs in *Timon of Athens*, and especially in the way that they fawn upon their masters, and she concludes that he used this as a metaphor for the worst kind of human relationship. In an essay called 'Timon's Dog',[30] William Empson examined this idea more closely, and decided that the dog image was made by Shakespeare to do double duty as a symbol of fawning but also of admirably snarling criticism of human weakness, as found in the sententiae of Jaques, Hamlet and Iago.[31] Shakespeare learned from Erasmus, Empson pointed out, that even in fawning a dog is being entirely sincere and faithful, and Empson uncovered a strain of dog-praising in *Timon of Athens* that Spurgeon had overlooked in her quantitative account. As a double symbol in the play, 'the dog does not manage to become a "symbol" that includes cynic and flatterer, flattery and affection, so as to imply a view of their proper relations. It remains a bridge over which they exchange puzzles.'[32]

It is currently fashionable to label such a literary or dramatic phenomenon as a kind of ambivalence and to value it as a barometer of unresolved tensions in a work, but for Empson the striking thing is that such symbolism 'could be worked out so far and yet remain somehow useless'.[33] It had its uses, though. In Shakespeare's *Julius Caesar*, at the moment of Mark Antony's apostrophe to the 'bleeding piece of earth' that is Caesar's murdered body, he imagines that Caesar's spirit will come 'hot from hell' and 'with a monarch's voice / Cry "havoc!" and let slip the dogs of war' (*Julius Caesar*, 3.1.275–6). The same dogs of war are given individual names in the prologue to Shakespeare's *Henry* V, where Harry is imagined holding the leashes of 'famine, sword, and fire' who 'Crouch for employment' (*Henry V*, Prologue, 7–8). In Shakespeare's last sole-authored play, as we shall see, such dangerous dogs under the control of a monarch's voice are actually brought onto the stage.

When Shakespeare's characters praise dogs, it is generally for their faithful ability to assist humans in hunting other animals, and how we read these moments depends on how we think hunting was perceived in the period. Spurgeon thinks that Shakespeare did not care for it: 'out of thirty-nine hunting images, I only once find the hunt pictured as a gay and joyous pastime'.[34] For contrast, she lists the many examples of Shakespeare's apparent delight in the behaviour of animals such as deer as expressed in his approval of their enjoyment of the safety of their natural habitats. We nonetheless have to make sense of apparently approving images of dogs in the service of hunters:

THESEUS
>My hounds are bred out of the Spartan kind,
>So flewed, so sanded; and their heads are hung
>With ears that sweep away the morning dew,
>Crook-kneed, and dewlapped like Thessalian bulls,
>Slow in pursuit, but matched in mouth like bells,
>Each under each. A cry more tuneable

Was never holla'd to nor cheered with horn
In Crete, in Sparta, nor in Thessaly.
Judge when you hear.
(*A Midsummer Night's Dream*, 4.1.118–26)

Stanley Wells argues that this exchange regarding the differing voices of the baying dogs illustrates the theme of unity-in-diversity, a concord or harmony that does not require sameness, 'an agreement that can include disagreement'.[35] The stage picture at this moment is of four sleeping lovers who were formerly at enmity, and the exchange of Theseus and Hippolyta about the 'musical confusion' of the pack of hounds is another way of expressing the reconciliation of the competing love interests.

This is a highly convincing argument in itself, but we might still be wary of the ideological significance of these visions of diversity. Leonard Tennenhouse observes that at this moment, when Theseus and Egeus discover the runaways Hermia and Lysander asleep together outside the city, the duke chooses to impute their behaviour to an artistic and submissive impulse rather than a seditious and disobedient one. 'No doubt,' he decides, 'they rose up early to observe / The rite of May, and, hearing our intent, / Came here in grace of our solemnity' (*A Midsummer Night's Dream*, 4.1.131–3). 'By identifying the lovers as revelers,' Tennenhouse points out, 'Theseus does more than decriminalize their transgression of the law; he identifies their state of disarray with the order of art .... What had been a violation of the father's law now becomes a scene of harmony.'[36] In other words, a supremely satisfying artistic image might well convey a disturbing political principle.

This all makes it rather difficult to assess Shakespeare's representations of animals. It is clear that only evil characters speak openly and casually of wanton violence towards sentient beings. Iago counsels Roderigo against suicide with mock incredulity: 'Drown thyself? Drown cats and blind puppies' (*Othello*, 1.3.335–6). The Queen tries to persuade Doctor Cornelius to give her poisons with the deceitful reassurance,

'I will try the forces / Of these thy compounds on such creatures as / We count not worth the hanging, but none human' (*Cymbeline*, 1.5.18–20). Cornelius sees through her, but thinks nothing wrong of her claimed intention 'In killing creatures vile, as cats and dogs / Of no esteem' (*Cymbeline*, 5.6.252–3), as he later reports it. We may turn away, then, from what is said of animals to consider just how they appear on the stage in Shakespeare's plays.

Only twice, at opposite ends of his career, does Shakespeare call for dogs to appear on his stage. The spirits that Prospero commands by way of Ariel take on the voices of dogs to sing the burden of the first of Ariel's songs:

ARIEL
  Come unto these yellow sands,
  …
  And, sweet sprites, bear
  The burden. Hark, hark.
SPIRITS
  (*dispersedly within*) Bow-wow!
ARIEL
  The watch-dogs bark.
SPIRITS
  (*within*) Bow-wow!
  (*The Tempest*, 1.2.377–86)

Caliban himself is sufficiently like a dog for Trinculo to call him a 'puppy-headed monster' (*The Tempest*, 2.2.153–4), and Eric C. Brown stresses his name's relationship to the word 'cannibal' that Christopher Columbus assumed was derived from the Latin root *canis* meaning dog.[37] Just what Ariel and Caliban looked like in the first performances is rather a difficult question to answer, for we have rather more evidence than is usually the case and it does not all point the same way.[38]

At the moment when his usurpation plot begins to fall because his human accomplices are distracted by gaudy clothing, Caliban is panic-stricken by the thought of being demoted still further down the Great Chain of Being: 'We shall ... all be turned to barnacles, or to apes / With foreheads villainous low' (*The Tempest*, 4.1.246–8). He is right to fear transformation, for the hunters shortly become the hunted:

A noise of hunters heard. Enter divers spirits in shape of dogs and hounds, hunting them about; Prospero and Ariel setting them on

PROSPERO
   Hey, Mountain, hey!

ARIEL
   Silver! There it goes, Silver!
PROSPERO
   Fury, Fury! There, Tyrant, there! Hark, hark!
   Exeunt Stefano, Trinculo, and Caliban, pursued by spirits
   (*The Tempest*, 4.1.254–5)

This moment is remarkable for the compliment it pays in treating Caliban as if he were the mythical hunter Actaeon, or, if he is puppy-headed, for the visually striking image of his own kind turning against him. Moreover, this urging on of his dogs is Prospero's only direct participation in the creation of terror, which is his main object throughout the play but which he has hitherto performed only by way of proxies.[39]

   At the other end of his career, Shakespeare had brought a dog on stage, and aside from the spirits-as-dogs in *The Tempest* he never repeated this feature of *The Two Gentlemen of Verona*. (On the assumption that early modern audiences enjoyed the dog as much as modern audiences do, Marc Norman and Tom Stoppard's script for the film *Shakespeare in Love* has Philip Henslowe object to the news of the omission from Shakespeare's next play with a disbelieving 'You mean, no dog of any kind?'[40]) The dog, Crab, appears in *The Two Gentlemen of Verona* always in the company of his master Lance, who himself appears only four times in the play, at 2.3.1–58, 2.5.1–51, 3.1.187–372 and, 4.4.1–59. Of these four entrances, Crab accompanies Lance on all but the penultimate one.

As a character, Crab exists to enable other characters, most often Lance, to draw parallels and contrasts between human behaviour and animal behaviour. To intensify the focus on this aspect of Crab's function, two of Lance's scenes, 2.3 and 4.4, begin as Lance's soliloquies about his dog. In the first, Lance describes Crab's failure to share the emotions of his family at his departure for Milan:

LANCE

> I think Crab, my dog, be the sourest-natured dog that lives. My mother weeping, my father wailing, my sister crying, our maid howling, our cat wringing her hands, and all our house in a great perplexity, yet did not this cruel-hearted cur shed one tear. He is a stone, a very pebble-stone, and has no more pity in him than a dog.
> (*The Two Gentlemen of Verona*, 2.3.5–11)

Lance simultaneously understands and does not understand the non-reaction of Crab, who as a dog 'has no more pity in him than a dog' and yet, for being that way, is called 'the sourest-natured dog that lives'. Crab's distance from the human world is emphasized in the contrast with the family cat, which has not only the feelings but the body parts ('hands') of the master species.

Behind this comic topic is the serious subject of this speech, which is about the communication of emotion. As Bruce R. Smith points out, the hydraulic theory of emotions – brilliantly summarized by Gail Kern Paster[41] – underpinned the early modern concept of how drama literally moves its audience:

> According to Galenic medicine, a person is who he or she is because of a distinctive balance of humors. The movements of those fluids throughout a person's person are experienced as 'passions' – or rather they are 'suffered' as passions ...

the actor deployed his control of passions in three distinct sites: in his own body, on the physical space around him, and on the ears and eyes of listeners/spectators. With respect to his own body, the actor had the power to induce in himself the physical passions that he wished to represent … [and according to Joseph] Roach, 'his motions could transform the air through which he moved, animating it in waves of force rippling outward from a center in his soul. His passions, irradiating the bodies of spectators through their eyes and ears, could literally transfer the contents of his heart to theirs, altering their moral natures'.[42]

In this view, emotion should be infectious and generate a kind of tidal sympathy between the rising fluids pouring out of the nose and eyes of the sufferer and a corresponding rise and overflow of the same fluids in the spectator.

Crab is immune to all this. Is that because he is a dog or because the scene of Lance leaving home was not sufficiently affecting? Exploring this question, the second half of Lance's speech is a curious examination of the mechanics of representation:

LANCE
Nay, I'll show you the manner of it. This shoe is my father. No, this left shoe is my father. No, no, this left shoe is my mother. Nay, that cannot be so, neither. Yes, it is so, it is so, it hath the worser sole. This shoe with the hole in it is my mother, and this my father. A vengeance on 't, there 'tis. Now, sir, this staff is my sister, for, look you, she is as white as a lily and as small as a wand. This hat is Nan our maid. I am the dog. No, the dog is himself, and I am the dog. O, the dog is me, and I am myself.
(*The Two Gentlemen of Verona*, 2.3.13–23)

Having already effectively conveyed the scene in words, Lance attempts to repeat it by ostension and finds that his properties are inadequate and easily confused with one another.

Moreover, two of his properties, himself and his dog, were themselves participants in the scene he is trying to convey and so they became entangled in a kind of ontological paradox, being equivalent to one another and to the subjects they are supposed to represent. If this is Shakespeare's first play, as is widely assumed on the basis of a dramatic awkwardness that might betray professional immaturity,[43] this soliloquy sounds rather like an accomplished poet – which Shakespeare already was – acknowledging that dramatic representation makes rather difficult what verbal dexterity makes easy. There are no truly affecting scenes in *The Two Gentlemen of Verona*, only the description of one that failed to affect.

Lance's second soliloquy with Crab develops further the first one's suggestion that man and beast might serve as models for one another. The occasion Lance describes is Crab's misbehaviour among 'three or four gentleman-like dogs' (*The Two Gentlemen of Verona*, 4.4.17), which begins with Crab's – presumably otherwise unnoticed – stealing of a capon's leg from Silvia's plate at dinner. When Crab urinates under the Duke's table, Lance takes the blame, and in complaining of this he recounts being stocked and pilloried for Crab's past offences (*The Two Gentlemen of Verona*, 4.4.18–32). At the level of overt expression, Lance and Crab are said to be interchangeable, and the same principle is working more subtly at the figurative level. Lance complains that 'a man's servant shall play the cur with him' (*The Two Gentlemen of Verona*, 4.4.1.2), which expression 'play the cur' meant to behave in an uncouth fashion. John Calvin preached that the Moabites and Ammonites had behaved like this towards the Israelites: they 'playde the barking curres and made hew and crie after them'.[44] Shakespeare's witticism is a short-circuiting of the metaphor: the cur Crab plays the cur because he is a cur.

Likewise, the metaphor 'to be dog at' something meant to be adept at it,[45] so that when Lance says he expects Crab 'to be, as it were, a dog at all things', including at being a dog (4.4.11–13), he is stating in one breath the highest possible expectation and also the mundane reality of the situation. He has split Crab into an impossible ideal of canine behaviour and an everyday failure to live up to that ideal. The characterological parallel for Lance's fidelity to his disappointing dog is Julia's fidelity to her disappointing lover Proteus, and it is to make this point about humans' expectations of one another that Shakespeare has Lance splitting Crab into idealized and ordinary beings. Lance has no more reason to object to the nature of his dog called Crab, 'the sourest-natured dog that lives' (2.3.5–6) because crabs were sour-tasting apples,[46] than Julia has to object to the changing nature of a man whose name, likewise, denotes just what he is: Proteus.

Beastliness

As ecocritics have repeatedly noted, Shakespeare's prime interest in humans' attitudes towards animals is the light that they shed on our sense of what it is to be human. The likenesses and contrasts between human characters and animals run across the drama. To denigrate someone it is required only to call him a dog, a boar or a chough; and to praise him it only takes to call him an eagle, a dolphin or a lion, each with their characteristic associated attributes. The creation of pairings that liken characters to one another and contrast them is a fundamental unit of dramatic creation, and indeed the Folio *dramatis personae* for *The Two Gentlemen of Verona* shows just how dependent upon this technique the early-career Shakespeare was. In it, except for the eponymous characters, everyone is defined by a relationship to someone else, most commonly using the preposition *to*:

Duke: Father to Siluia.
...
Thurio: a foolish riuall to Valentine.

...
Speed: a clownish seruant to Valentine.
Launce: the like to Protheus.

...
Lucetta: waighting woman to Iulia.[47]

We do not know where the Folio's various *dramatis personae* lists come from, although the outer wrappers that were used to hold together a bundle of actors' parts for each play might usefully have such lists written upon them. If so, we here get a sense of how the play was conceived from the practical point of view of casting it, the type of a character being conveniently summarized by such a list.

The *dramatis personae* for *The Two Gentlemen of Verona* asserts that Speed is '*a clownish seruant*' to Valentine, and Lance is '*the like to Protheus*'. This is misleading, for Lance and Speed are unlike as clownish servants. Speed frequently gets the better of his master, having a keener understanding of what is going on, for example, in Silvia's commissioning Valentine to write her a love letter. Lance, however, is in the familiar mould of clowns such as the Dromios from *The Comedy of Errors*, or Dogberry from *Much Ado About Nothing*. Moreover, with two extensive soliloquies and almost no interaction with other characters, Lance's part is distinct and detachable from the rest of the play and might well have been written later. Yet this *dramatis personae*, which must have been written after the play was completed, insists that Lance is '*like*' Speed, collapsing a pair of binary relations into a single model of clownish service.

It seems that wherever this play attempts to hold apart the elements of a contrast – human/human and human/animal – the paradoxes of performance collapse them into sameness: 'the dog is me, and I am myself' (*The Two Gentlemen of Verona*, 2.3.21–2). For all that the play tries to distinguish Speed and Lance, confusion of identities pervades it from the beginning. In the very first scene, we find that Speed (Valentine's man) rather than Lance (Proteus' man) was, before the start of the play, commissioned to carry Proteus' letter to Julia. Such ineluctable two-in-oneness was yet another aspect of Shakespeare's earliest work to which he returned in his very last work. In *The Two Noble Kinsmen*, collaboratively written with John Fletcher in 1613–14, Shakespeare again used a titular pairing to explore the difference of man and man.

In Shakespeare, the word *beast* and its cognates (*beastly*, *beastliness* and so on) are most frequently used in the tragedies (about five times per play, or four if we exclude the anomalous *Timon of Athens*), next most frequently used in the comedies (nearly three times per play) and least used in the histories (twice per play). The commonest reason to compare humans to beasts is to condemn the humans for sinking to the beasts' level of existence, typically in showing a lack of compassion, or in giving in to base desires (lusts and appetites) rather than overcoming them by dint of Reason. For example, seeing the drunken Christopher Sly on the ground, the Lord in *The Taming of the Shrew* is disgusted: 'O monstrous beast! How like a swine he lies' (Induction, 1.32). But sometimes the purpose of the comparison is to give humans something to live up to, as when Hamlet, reciting a speech he has learned, likens 'rugged Pyrrhus' to the 'Hyrcanian beast', a kind of tiger. As Ann Thompson and Neil Taylor remark, this associates Pyrrhus with 'heroic action, unlike the negative associations of *beast*' elsewhere in the play.[48]

This doubled meaning latent in the notion of being beast-like could be used in one of Shakespeare's favourite tricks of making a character find in what someone has just said a punning secondary meaning, and then find that this second meaning is in fact more appropriate to the dramatic context than the primary meaning intended by the speaker. Thus, when the Queen upbraids Richard II for accepting his defeat by Bolingbroke, she reminds him, 'thou … art a lion and the king of beasts'. In response, Richard intentionally misunderstands the word *of* to mean not *amongst* but *ruling over*: 'A king of beasts indeed! If aught but beasts, / I had been still a happy king of men' (*Richard II*, 5.1.31–6).

In such punning we see evidence to suppose that for Shakespeare there is no single, fixed and unproblematic essence to the human/beast relationship. Rather, like so much else in Shakespeare's world, the relationship is open to challenge and is actively contested as part of the wider struggle for meanings within the events being dramatized. Richard seems to accept finally that, no matter that much of the ideology of kingship makes him a lion among beasts, the reality of kingship cannot transform those beasts to make them conform to his will. But our sense that this is what Richard has finally come to accept at the end of the play is a trick Shakespeare plays on us, since Richard was comprehensively taught this lesson in the play's opening scene.

Attempting to coerce Thomas Mowbray into dropping his accusations against Henry Bolingbroke, Richard reminds him: 'Lions make leopards tame', to which Mowbray replies: 'Yea, but not change his spots' (*Richard II*, 1.1.175–6). There may be some complex punning here on the derivation of the word leopard – *leo* (lion) crossed with a *pard* – but most clearly this refusal by Mowbray to be made tame invokes an essentialist principle. That is, there remains an unalterable hard reality to the existence of animals, howsoever we try to co-opt their characteristics to our ideological ends. In another of Shakespeare's recurrent explorations of the Nature/Nurture debate, or, to put this in the conventional terms of Literary Theory, the essentialism/constructivism debate, Shakespeare here uses an essentialist principle to teach Richard a hard lesson. He takes the whole play to learn it.

structures that our internal organs can process. Even if we confine ourselves to cells in our bodies that contain a single human DNA sequence, those that we think of as being quintessentially 'ourselves', the mere fact that they work together for the collective good of something of which they comprise only a part – the human body – is itself an extraordinary act of collaboration that gives us a model for larger collaborative bodies.[1]

One of the conceptual problems in moving between levels of interest – from cells to individuals, from individuals to collectives – is that wholes really can be more than the sums of their parts. The phenomena we are interested in may be what is called emergent because they are not present in any of the parts but arise only from the interactions between parts. Language is the archetypal emergent phenomenon, since, although a word bears meaning, it is clear that this meaning does not reside in any of the letters which the word comprises. Rather, the meaning arises from the specific combination of letters. The self-regulation of Gaia is an emergent phenomenon and is not attributable to any particular part of the system.

As we saw in Chapter 2, Richard Dawkins' popularizations of neoDarwinism were designed to shift attention away from individual organisms and take up the perspective of their genes, so that he could show, among other things, that what looks like selfless behaviour at the level of the individual is in fact selfish behaviour at the level of the gene. Unfortunately, this necessary readjustment made Dawkins blind to the emergent property of planetary self-regulation and led to his mockery of James Lovelock's hypothesis. Why would creatures act selflessly for planetary regulation, why would their genes encourage this behaviour, asked Dawkins? The answer is that no one particular creature is doing this; the phenomenon exists only at the level of the larger system.

In the same way, no particular cell or group of cells in my body is being 'me' right now. Rather, I am the expression of their collective activity. I am quite happy to lose thousands of cells every day – shed from skin, recycled in my internal processes – without feeling that any part of me is lost. Indeed, the very failure of individual cells to die when I need them to constitutes a threat to my continued existence, since this is what we mean by cancerous tumours. A solitary ant is much like a solitary human cell, in that it has no genetic future – it cannot reproduce – and being utterly specialized it cannot survive on its own for any substantial period of time without all the other specialists that make up the colony.

The queen of an ant colony could be seen as misnamed, since she is more like a reproductive organ of an individual than a ruler of a kingdom. The particular circumstances in which an ant colony finds itself are likely to make different kinds of collective, colony-wide behaviour more or less advantageous to its growth. Under some circumstances a colony may find itself in situations that reward aggressive foraging; in others, situations that punish aggressive foraging and promote cautious forays beyond the well-protected nest. Remarkably, evidence is emerging that an entire colony may have, as it were, its own personality regarding such behaviours.[2] In the same way that individuals in solitary species differ from one another in their personalities – their preference for aggressive or defensive behaviour, their willingness to take risks – so too do whole ant colonies.

Among the many remarkable things about insect colonies that exhibit behaviour we have long associated with higher animals is that there is no obvious centre from which this behaviour is coordinated. Although the queen ant can be likened to a higher animal's sexual organs, there is nothing in the colony that corresponds to a brain. Equally, a number of ecological systems are regulated without central control, and indeed this is what we mean by the behaviour being emergent for the system. The largest man-made system that operates without central control is the Internet, which was specifically designed to operate by distributed rules because this approach would make it resistant to disruption by mechanical failure or deliberate attack.[3]

At the core of this planet-wide system is a set of protocols – that is, computer behaviours – called Transmission

Control Protocol/Internet Protocol (TCP/IP) that regulate the movement of the units of computer data, called packets, from machine to machine. Two novel principles have enabled the Internet to succeed as a planet-wide system: the allocation of the data to be moved into these discrete packets, travelling independently of one another across the network, and the absence of coordination by any central authority, leaving the route they take to be decided by information, itself distributed across the network, about which routes are open. In a very real sense, a packet has to find its way across the Internet much as a foraging ant has to hunt for food.

When determining how many ants to send out foraging on any particular occasion, ant colonies rely on how many ants are successfully returning from foraging. When many foragers are returning with food, more are sent out, and when few are returning the rate of sending out fresh foragers declines. The rate of return of foraging expeditions is an index of how much food is available, and by modulating the outgoing stream of ants the collective effort is tuned to match the success rate.[4] This evolved behaviour happens at the level of the individual forager ant deciding whether to leave, and it uses the same algorithm by which the Transmission Control Protocol of the Internet manages the flow of packets of information between two computers that are exchanging data. The faster the acknowledgements come back indicating successful delivery of previous packets, the faster fresh packets are sent out to take advantage of the available bandwidth. The algorithm raises the rate of transmission until the rate of return shows that the available bandwidth is optimally used, just as the colony raises the rate of outgoing foragers to optimally exploit the available food. All of this takes place without central planning.

When this discovery about ants was first made public in 2012, journalists hit upon the name Anternet to encapsulate it, and for the most part they reflected that it made a mockery of human vanity in thinking that the Internet is an extraordinary invention: after all, the ants got there first, and many millennia before we did. This is, however, entirely the wrong way to view the delightful correspondence of the ants' algorithm and our own, because in fact the discovery reflects most handsomely on our achievement. It took evolution millions of years to come up with the ants' algorithm by the utterly wasteful process of blindly trying every possible solution and throwing away (by natural selection) all those that did not work. By contrast, once humans put their minds to the problem they homed in on the solution in a few years and then broadcast the solution in the form of technical papers for all to copy. This neatly illustrates Dawkins' point that replicating entities need not be biological. Once Earth had developed a species capable of complex language (us), cultural replicators that Dawkins christened 'memes' could do what biological evolution achieves, but we could do it much more quickly and efficiently.[5]

Theatre crowds

When thinking about how individuals come together to form crowds, we should reflect that the very existence of the early modern theatre depended upon turning crowds into audiences. The virtually circular design of the open-air playhouses represents the fairest way for a given number of people to be placed at a minimal distance from an object of common visual interest. Indeed, this is one of the ways of defining a circle algorithmically. The walls and internal barriers of an open-air amphitheatre playhouse gave the performers the best way of ensuring that all who watched the performance paid for doing so, and it allowed for some useful variation in the quality and hence the price of the accommodation on offer: standing for a penny, seated for two.[6]

Evelyn Tribble shows that the structure of the early modern theatre acted as a kind of mental prosthesis that enabled the actors to perform prodigious feats of memory in reciting hundreds of lines of dialogue that changed, as the play being shown changed, every day.[7] It should also be acknowledged that the building itself worked upon the crowd that entered it to become an audience, by engaging each person in a trans-action and by regulating his or her behaviour.

It is quite likely that theatre audiences retained much of a crowd-like demeanour for all that. Open-air theatres were notoriously rowdy places and the efforts of civic authorities to close them frequently focused on the lawlessness and public nuisance they caused. Because the audience in the playhouse yard was standing, it was potentially mobile and physically reactive to events around the venue as well as those on stage. The contract for the building of the Fortune open-air playhouse in 1600 called for spiked railings to be placed around the yard wall ('fenced wth stronge yron pykes') to keep the standing audience securely contained within this perimeter.[8] The Fortune contract explicitly takes as its model the Globe playhouse built the year before, so we have somehow to reconcile these physical arrangements with an understanding that Shakespeare's finest dramatic verse was addressed to such audiences. Just how did a play get started under these seemingly adverse, rowdy conditions?

Tiffany Stern's convincing answer is that unless the play was already an established hit then much of the preparatory work was done by the prologue, and the audience was given the power to reject a play or have it changed.[9] According to Stern, the first performance of a new play had a special function, because if the play failed to please on that occasion in all likelihood it would not be offered again, and the prologue was a one-off speech written for this special occasion in response to this pressure. Playwrights had a financial imperative in writing these prologues, because, although they were paid a fee for the delivered script, they could also expect a so-called benefit performance – typically the second or third showing – in which they were entitled to a share of the playhouse take. If a play did not survive the first performance, this additional income was lost to the playwright. Empowering the spectators, then, was one of the ways by which theatre companies managed expectations and turned the theatre's crowd into an audience.

This audience could, at dramatic need, be turned back into a crowd for the purpose of standing for one in the play. This trick solved the problem that the actors simply could not easily summon enough bodies onto the stage to present realistically a large crowd. Richard's and Richmond's orations to their armies in *Richard III* are typical of moments that are likely to have deployed this technique (5.5.190–224, 5.6.44–81). An alternative way to suggest the existence of crowds was to pretend that they were behind one of the stage doors and trying but failing to burst onto the stage. This is the technique that Shakespeare uses in *Hamlet*, when Polonius' son returns to Elsinore from Paris on hearing of his father's death:

> ... young Laertes, in a riotous head,
> O'erbears your officers. The rabble call him lord,
> ...
> They cry 'Choose we! Laertes shall be king'.
> (*Hamlet*, 4.5.99–104)

This is accompanied by loud noises '*within*' that signal the rabble's riotousness, and then:

> *Enter Laertes* [*with his followers at the door*]
> LAERTES
>   Where is the King? – Sirs, stand you all without.
> ALL HIS FOLLOWERS
>   No, let's come in.
> LAERTES
>   I pray you, give me leave.
> ALL HIS FOLLOWERS
>   We will, we will.
> LAERTES
>   I thank you. Keep the door. [*Exeunt followers*] O thou
>   vile king...
>   (*Hamlet*, 4.5.109–14)

To have only a few actors trying to push through the stage door to accompany Laertes onto the stage would suggest many more unseen behind them. Laertes' instruction to 'keep the door' – meaning let no one else onto the stage through this door – gives a justification for these few actors closing the door behind them, and the audience may then imagine them fulfilling his command on its far side.

For Gertrude, the disorderliness of this crowd is reminiscent of the disorderliness into which hunting with dogs may descend if not expertly handled. 'How cheerfully on the false trail they cry!' she remarks, and then, after '*A noise within*', 'O, this is counter, you false Danish dogs!' (*Hamlet*, 4.5.107–8). The scent ('trail') of a hunted animal leads in two directions – whence it came and where it is running to – and in following the trail to Claudius the rabble ('dogs') and their leader Laertes are going in precisely the wrong direction. This is a startlingly partisan image for Gertrude to use, since the opposite direction must lead towards her son Hamlet, whom she knows to be the quarry they seek if Polonius' death is to be revenged. Importantly, for our purposes, the components of the rabble are merely dogs and the control of them lies in their leader, Laertes.

Much the same device of an implied offstage crowd is used towards the end of Shakespeare's and John Fletcher's play *Henry VIII* (5.3) to depict a potentially dangerous gathering of Londoners seeking to break onto the stage to witness the christening of the infant Princess Elizabeth (later Queen Elizabeth). There is much fun had as the Porter and his Man ekphrastically conjure up the offstage scenes of confrontation that have supposedly just occurred; but the occasion is essentially celebratory rather than seditious. And, unlike the rabble in *Hamlet*, this one has no leader: each person has come for the essentially loyal, if boisterous, purpose of witnessing the future queen's first public ceremony. (That she would become queen was, of course, by no means certain during the reign of King Henry VIII being depicted, but everyone watching the play's first performances in 1613 knew that she had come to the throne.) Also, there is no likening of this crowd to animals as there was of the rabble in *Hamlet*.

It is commonly asserted that in his crowd scenes Shakespeare shows a conservative fear of mass movements and direct political action. The truth is rather more subtle than that. His play, *Coriolanus,* starts with the entry of '*a company of mutinous Citizens with staves, clubs, and other weapons*' who, it turns out, suspect that the Roman aristocrats, and Caius Martius in particular, are hoarding grain, and that the present famine is essentially man-made rather than natural. As Michael Warren points out, the behaviour of this crowd in almost all modern editions of the play is rather different from its behaviour in our only textual authority for the play, the 1623 Folio.[10] In the Folio, the First Citizen is the first to speak and he lays out the accusations against Caius Martius at length until, a couple of minutes into the play, Menenius Agrippa enters and addresses the citizens. At this point, the First Citizen falls silent and the grievances of the crowd are laid out to Menenius by the Second Citizen. This passing of the baton, as it were, from the First to the Second Citizen is usually removed in modern editions, on the grounds that it is implausible for the scene-opening hothead to suddenly fall silent.

Michael Warren argues, however, that this reassignment has the undesirable effect of making the Roman crowd seem homogeneous and led by a single agitator, while the Folio's dispersal of lines makes the crowd polyvocal and more intelligent because it comprises a consort of voices in agreement. Although Warren does not mention it, we may well think that such a coordinated yet diverse crowd is not unlike the collection of coordinated yet diverse cells in a multicellular organism, resembling, too, the coordinated diversity of advanced human societies.

For Warren, there is an important character distinction to be made: in the Folio, the First Citizen is anti-authoritarian, while the Second Citizen is conciliatory, and changes his views as the crowd's grievances are aired. Warren's argument persuaded Peter Holland to retain the Folio's speech prefixes in his Arden3 edition of the play and to give credence to the wording of the Folio's stage direction: this is a 'company' of 'Citizens', not a mob.[11] That is, Holland accepted the civic nature of what previous editors tended to think of as a mere mob.

Of special concern to us, of course, is the fact that editors make the First Citizen a ringleader, while the Folio's company is composed of individuals thinking through their situation collectively. As Holland rightly notes, far from representing the coming of democracy, the appointment of the tribunes is politically regressive:

> After the tribunes are in place as the 'tongues o'th' common mouth' (3.1.22), the people are shown to be manipulable. What is more, as the tribunes speak for them, so the people speak little, effectively silenced with their voices largely taken away. Having been vocal in the first scene, speaking half the lines before Caius Martius' entrance, they speak surprisingly infrequently in the whole rest of the play, barely as many as they have spoken in 1.1, while Brutus and Sicinius are substantial roles, nearly 500 lines combined.[12]

In a moment of self-mockery, the Third Citizen later agrees with Caius Martius' characterization of the company as a 'many-headed multitude' since their 'wits are so diversely coloured' (*Coriolanus*, 2.3.16–20), but this can hardly be a criticism if the contrast to mob-rule is thinking for oneself.

Nonetheless, crowds in Shakespeare do behave badly. Since Shakespeare was a poet, we have to suppose that the tearing to pieces of Cinna the Poet in *Julius Caesar* was a moment he felt particularly keenly in the writing (3.3.27–38). The Folio text, again our only authority, does not provide a stage direction for this action, but it is certainly implied in the language of the plebians: 'Tear him' is said five times by three different speakers. In performance this repeated cry may be ironized by the crowd's saying it but not carrying it out, and, as David Daniell reports (with strong disapproval), this was routine on the Anglo-American stage between 1817 and 1937.[13] This is a crowd that has been shown to be fickle, initially backing Caesar's assassins, and then, under the influence of Antony's rhetoric, turning against them.

Divided loyalties and collective actions

At about the same time as writing the scene depicting this Roman crowd whipped into a violent frenzy by Antony's words, Shakespeare wrote almost exactly its opposite: a scene of an English crowd being talked down from violent frenzy to peaceful submission by Thomas More. The play, *Sir Thomas More,* tells of the rise of the historical figure More (1478–1535), who goes from being one of the two undersheriffs of London to becoming a knight and privy counsellor, and finally to the Lord Chancellorship, one of the highest government offices in England, bringing him close to King Henry VIII. The second half of the play charts More's fall from power, arising from his refusal to sign a document accepting Henry VIII's assertion of himself as the head of the newly formed Church of England. The service that gains More his greatest promotion in the first half of the play is the quelling of a riot against foreigners accused by Londoners of harming their trades and of public disorders including the abduction of women.

The play does not name or depict the king and does not make specific the circumstances of More's moral dilemma – it comes down to whether to obey his king or his religious conscience – so presumably these details were thought to be well known to playgoers. More's book, *Utopia*, written in Latin and first published in 1516, had been published in three English-language editions by the time the play was written, and his fame appears to have been widespread. In particular, More's role in the calming of a riot against foreigners in London (the so-called Ill May Day uprising of 1517), dramatized in Shakespeare's contribution to the play, was topical in the 1590s as xenophobic tensions rose in the capital.

The rioters, some of them in armour, seek out the foreigners' houses and discuss how to deal with the state forces that they know are being mustered against them. The foreigners' houses are discovered to be empty – they had earlier fled in fear – so the rioters decide to set fire to them and make good their escape while the Lord Mayor is organizing his men to put out the fires. As John Jowett observes, this parallels the burning of the houses of the conspirators in *Julius Caesar*.[14] More discovers that some of the rioters have broken open the prisons and swelled their insurrection with the criminals they have released, and he proposes a parley with the riot's ringleaders. Approaching the rioters, More rescues a sergeant-at-arms whom they are attacking and he calls on them to listen to him.

That Shakespeare consciously or unconsciously linked the rabble-raising scene he wrote in *Julius Caesar* with the rabble-quelling scene he wrote in *Sir Thomas More* is clear from the phrasing of the first attempt to parley with them. The Earl of Surrey begins with 'Friends, masters, countrymen' (*Sir Thomas More*, 6.32), which parallels Antony's 'Friends, Romans, countrymen' (*Julius Caesar*, 3.2.74) in precisely the same situation of calling for a noisy crowd to settle, pay attention and listen. Where Antony succeeds, Surrey fails. More approaches the problem by assuming that the crowd has leadership and he appeals to it: 'You that have voice and credit with the number, / Command them to a stillness' (*Sir Thomas More*, 6.61). John Lincoln, who is later hanged as one of the ringleaders, responds that this is impossible, but after Doll Williamson's approval of More the crowd begins calling for silence with 'Peace, peace!' As More remarks, calling out for silence is self-defeating: 'Look what you do offend you cry upon / That is, the peace', and Jowett suggests that the phrase 'cry upon' might convey 'an ironic suggestion of hounds in cry after their prey'.[15]

The comparison of humans to animals comes up again in More's argument that should mere might prevail in the matter of the foreigners' behaviour no one is safe, since 'other ruffians', taking this rebellion as their precedent, 'Would shark on you, and men, like ravenous fishes, / Would feed on one another' (*Sir Thomas More*, 6.95–8). If the king were to banish the rebels for their rebellion, they would become foreigners in a strange land and, on the present example, the natives could with justice 'Spurn you like dogs' (*Sir Thomas More*, 6.150). Unlike the uprising in *Julius Caesar*, the rebellion in *Sir Thomas More* in no way threatens the way that the city or the country is governed. If the rebels had any such grand plans for fundamental change – even if only to change monarchs, as is the aim of Laertes' supporters in *Hamlet* – then More's image of the consequences of the king banishing them would hold no terrors for them.

More's images of violated order are at their most vivid when he says that the rebels are leading the 'majesty of law in lyam', that is tied up with a leash: 'To slip him like a hound' (*Sir Thomas More*, 6.137–8). The threat the crowd poses is, ultimately, one of decorum not of political substance: the rebels are taking justice into their own hands when it properly belongs to the king and his deputies, including More. Their rebellion against the foreigners, More argues, is really a rebellion against their king. In the event, More is easily able to talk this crowd out of its ambitions by implying the Christian Golden Rule, leaving it to the pens to name it explicitly: 'Let's do as we may be done by' (*Sir Thomas More*, 6.157–8).

The entire action of this scene is, of course, in retrospect, ironized by More's later response to the dilemma he faces when his king asks him to subscribe to a religious principle, the Act of [monarchical] Supremacy, that More is unable to accept. At this stage in the play More rhetorically and oratorically wields to great effect the idea that monarchical and religious powers naturally form an alliance, in that the king is God's deputy. Ironically, Henry's Act of Supremacy could plausibly be defended as a strengthening of this alliance, since the king would then in one person represent the highest temporal and spiritual authority, while, under the arrangements that More dies defending, the monarch is the highest temporal authority but the Pope in Rome is the highest spiritual authority. This division of authority adds a complexity that More does not present to the rioting Londoners, a rhetorical aporia that playgoers are doubtless intended to consider. A model of order based on appeal to the natural emergence of social hierarchies that gives to parts of society (typically, classes) their assigned place within the whole tends to unravel when there co-exist two official hierarchies at odds with one another.

The play *Sir Thomas More* hammers this point home by showing a grave injustice arising from yet another pair of competing hierarchies, those of monarchical authority and London City authority. This tension is dramatized twice in each of two public executions. Royal clemency for the rebels was the chief precondition for their acceptance of More's plea to disarm and let themselves be arrested. As Lincoln says: 'We'll be ruled by you, Master / More, if you'll stand our friend to procure our pardon' (*Sir Thomas More*, 6.159–60). The play leaves unresolved uncertainty about just why the execution of the rebels nonetheless proceeds, but key culpability seems to lie with the Master Sheriff who tells his men 'be speedy … make haste … and see no time be slacked' (7.10–14). Behind all this is the division of authority between the London Corporation (the City) and the monarch in Westminster.

As an ordinary matter of civil unrest inside the city walls, the riot comes under the jurisdiction of the London authorities, but the Crown may be appealed to as the ultimate arbiter on all matters within the realm. More makes just such an appeal to Henry VIII, while the City continues with the legal process. The division of authority between the monarch and the City also resonates with the division of authority between the king as temporal leader and the Pope as spiritual leader. Or, to see it as the dramatists and their intended first audiences would perhaps have seen it, the dramatization of the split authority in London – which is the dramatic motor of the execution scenes – offered a way to glance at the fundamental split in authority that the play cannot openly name but which is central to the story of More's downfall.

In his gallows speech, Lincoln refers to the foreigners who 'wronged us overmuch' (*Sir Thomas More*, 7.54) but immediately acknowledges that the state has the monopoly on righting such wrongs: 'it was not fit / That private men should carve out their redress / Which way they list' (*Sir Thomas More*, 7.55–7). To seek private redress is to undermine 'Obedience', which he points out is a principle governing not only the ordinary people but 'each degree' (*Sir Thomas More*, 7.58); that is, every social class. Although the Master Sheriff is the highest ranking official present, the lesson is applicable to the recently knighted former sheriff, More, who, this scene later reveals, has, for his pleading on behalf of the rioters, been elevated to Lord Chancellor.

Shockingly, no pardon comes for the rebels and Lincoln climbs the scaffold and '*leaps off*' (*Sir Thomas More*, 7.69). The theatre audience must wonder if More had simply lied about attempting to secure the king's mercy for the ringleaders, or else had tried and failed. In her execution speech that follows Lincoln's, Doll Williamson is explicitly disappointed in More: 'Yet would I praise his honesty much more / If he had kept his word and saved our lives' (*Sir Thomas More*, 7.102–3). Pardon comes just in time to save Doll, but too late for Lincoln, and to that extent More has indeed broken his word as given to Lincoln, and somewhat loses the audience's sympathy.

In his transition from servant of London to servant of the Crown, More is acutely conscious of leaving his old friends and masters behind. Thus, in Scene 9, when More is visited at home by the Lord Mayor and alderman he is awkwardly at pains to deny that elevation had changed him:

MORE
    Once again, welcome, welcome, my good Lord Mayor,
    And brethren all – for once I was your brother,

> And so am still in heart. It is not state
> That can our love from London separate.
> (*Sir Thomas More*, 9.92–5)

There follow polite but pained disagreements about who should sit where for the entertainment that More provides.

To understand the significance of the tension between the City and the court requires some knowledge of the geopolitics and economics of early modern London. The river formed a natural southern boundary to the authority of the City, with the land on the south bank coming under the jurisdiction of the magistrates of Surrey and, in part, the Bishop of Winchester, although Southwark (where the open-air playhouses were located) was annexed as a suburb of the City in 1550.[16] Although the monarch was the ultimate ruler and authority in early modern England, London had considerable economic autonomy, with all trade being regulated by the City Corporation not the Crown.

The division of authority between the City and Crown is literalized in the staging at the beginning of the final scene, More's execution. The scene's opening stage direction is '[*A scaffold is set forth.*] *Enter the* [*two*] *Sheriffs of London and their Officers at one door, the Warders with their halberds at another*' (*Sir Thomas More*, 17.0). The Warders are the guards of the Tower of London and halberds are their weapons. The Tower of London was one of the palaces owned by the monarch. It is situated at the south-eastern corner of the fortified wall that marked the boundary of the City, where it meets the Thames, and thus is a liminal space where the authority of City and Crown interact. The Crown had independent access to the Tower of London because it could be reached by river, and More is said to be arriving that way at the start of scene 14. The Tower was so strongly associated with its river access that in More's Wife's nightmare the couple are sucked into a whirlpool on the Thames just in front of the Tower (*Sir Thomas More*, 11.8–26).

Although More is guilty of an offence against the Crown, in

the final scene it is the City that must execute him, and hence its opening stage direction prepares for his being handed back to the sheriffs after imprisonment by the Crown in the Tower of London. The stage of an open-air amphitheatre playhouse of Shakespeare's time thrust out into the yard where the audience stood and was backed by a wall pierced by two stage doors, with possibly a larger central opening and/or discovery space between them. By having the sheriffs enter at one of these doors, and the Tower of London's guards enter at the other, to start the final scene, the play emblematizes this polarity of power. The theatre stage stands as the space where the authority of the monarch meets that of the City.

As Janette Dillon explores, the tension between the City and monarchical authority was a recurrent focus of drama in Shakespeare's time and was unavoidable even in plays that are not explicitly about this tension, as *Sir Thomas More* is.[17] The wider question these plays raise is to whom exactly one's loyalties are due. An early modern London playgoer might feel loyalty to his trade and guild, to London, to England and to his religious faith, which might not be English Protestantism. The first of these competing loyalties, to one's trade, is dramatized in the opening scene of *Julius Caesar* when the '*certain commoners*' reveal themselves as carpenter and cobbler and are berated for not wearing the clothes that make these trades apparent. It does not occur to Flavius and Murellus, who berate them for their appearance, to celebrate the commoners' apparent choice, in their dress, to self-identify as all Romans together rather than as various kinds of tradesmen subdivided by their occupations.

The family versus social networks

Among Shakespeare's earliest plays is a sequence concerned with a crisis in the system by which Englishmen identified their allegiances, the so-called War of the Roses. These plays ask the highly pertinent question of just which larger body politic an individual should identify as the one to which he should primarily consider himself affiliated. The aristo-cratic warlords of the history plays are, effectively, local monarchs with their own courts, and the struggle for power in these plays is primarily between these local leaders and the monarchy as a centralized authority. Among the aristocrats, the separation into two opposed armed groups – supporters of the Lancastrians (wearing red roses) and of the Yorkists (wearing white roses) – arises in Shakespeare's depiction not from long-standing historical or regional allegiances but from disagreement over a point of principle.

The key scene depicting this disagreement begins with the entrance of several aristocrats as if leaving London's Temple Hall, where its lawyers congregated, and entering the Hall's garden. An unnamed legal question is in dispute between Richard Plantagenet and the Duke of Somerset, and the Earls of Suffolk and Warwick declare it too complex for them. Their refusal to judge may be disingenuous, as Richard Plantagenet suggests:

RICHARD PLANTAGENET
    Since you are tongue-tied and so loath to speak,
    In dumb significants proclaim your thoughts.
    Let him that is a true-born gentleman
    And stands upon the honour of his birth,
    If he suppose that I have pleaded truth,
    From off this briar pluck a white rose with me.
    He plucks a white rose
SOMERSET
    Let him that is no coward nor no flatterer,
    But dare maintain the party of the truth,
    Pluck a red rose from off this thorn with me.
    He plucks a red rose
    (*Henry VI, Part One*, 2.4.25–33)

Most commentators agree that *Henry VI, Part One* was written after what are now called the second and third parts, to which it forms a prequel. If the idea of having the two factions identify themselves by wearing blossoms from a rose brier was invented by Shakespeare only after writing the earlier plays, it seems to have caused those plays to then be revised to incorporate this detail, since the first edition of *Henry VI, Part Three* starts with the Yorkist faction entering 'with white Roses in their hats', followed shortly thereafter by the Lancastrians 'with red Roses in their hats'.[18]

As the others choose their roses in the Temple Garden scene, it occurs to Vernon that this show of allegiances might be turned into a kind of democratic poll: 'he upon whose side / The fewest roses from the tree are cropped / Shall yield the other in the right opinion' (*Henry VI, Part One*, 2.4.40–2). The protagonists agree, but when the white roses predominate Somerset refuses to be bound by the agreement. The dispute is as yet unnamed in the play but it clearly involves Richard Plantagenet's forebears' relationship with the monarchy. With Edmund Mortimer's revelations in the next scene, it becomes apparent that Richard Plantagenet has a claim to the throne of England arising from the usurpation of Richard II by his cousin Henry Bolingbroke (Henry IV), grandfather to the present king Henry VI. The larger story of the three plays about Henry VI is that his political weakness enables Richard Plantagenet to pursue his claim successfully, to the extent of putting his son on the throne as Edward IV.

This then is a series of plays concerned, as is *Sir Thomas More*, with power as it is regionally based in cities and counties (York, Lancaster, Suffolk, Somerset) versus the centralized power of the monarchy. The plays dramatize the competing demands upon English men and women of having a local authority and a central one, and recurrently they bring in the additional demand of family loyalty as an alternative to either. Indeed, one of the most affecting scenes in the cycle, *Henry VI, Part Three*, 2.5, is a dramatization of a soldier who carries in the dead body of an opponent he has killed only to remove the helmet and discover that it is his own father. Immediately afterwards, another soldier enters and the action is repeated to reveal that this one has killed his only son. The idea of family loyalties and the defence of children runs across the history play as a counterpoint to the regional and national loyalties they show coming into conflict.

In *Henry VI, Part One*, the great warrior Talbot and his son John are caught in a military disaster near Bordeaux that will clearly end with the death of anyone who fails to fly. Each tries to persuade the other to save himself by leaving. The son's argument is that his very filial relationship is at stake:

> JOHN
>   Is my name Talbot, and am I your son,
>   And shall I fly? O, if you love my mother,
>   Dishonour not her honourable name
>   To make a bastard and a slave of me.
>   The world will say he is not Talbot's blood
>   That basely fled when noble Talbot stood.
>   (*Henry VI, Part One*, 4.5.12–17)

John argues that his father Talbot should fly because the elder man's great honour already earned cannot be lost and because the French would make much propaganda from the death of so renowned a warrior, yet could make nothing of the death of his as-yet-untried son. Talbot's response is: 'Part of thy father may be saved in thee', and: 'Thou never hadst renown, nor canst not lose it' (*Henry VI, Part One*, 4.5.38, 40). Why cannot they both fly? Talbot's response makes clear the conflict between family loyalty and the larger social grouping to which he has attached importance: '[TALBOT] And leave my followers here to fight and die? / My age was never tainted with such shame' (*Henry VI, Part One*, 4.5.45).

Not until Shakespeare had created at least ten plays did he, in *Romeo and Juliet*, manage to produce a tragedy that did not essentially depend on the conflict between familial bonds and a soldier's duty to the wider social group – the faction, the city, the empire – to which he has aligned himself. According to Scott McMillin and Sally-Beth MacLean, the history play genre, which apparently gave Shakespeare his start in the theatre industry, was itself developed by the Queen's Men's playing company in the 1580s precisely in order to promote the cause of national Protestant unity – which was the Earl of Leicester's and Francis Walsingham's intention in putting the company together.[19] If so, in Shakespeare's hands – and those of his collaborators in the Henry VI plays, none of which was solely Shakespeare's work – the genre became considerably more subtle in its portrayal of the causes and consequences of competing loyalties.

Every Shakespeare comedy is about the creation of the smallest social structure that is chosen rather than given: the marital pair. Of course, the coming together of these pairs creates families and thus parent–child relationships that are not chosen but given by biology. As we saw in Chapter 2, not until near the end of his career did Shakespeare explore the complexities of the family relationships that follow marriage, and in particular the effects of adoption and procreative uncertainty. When marriages become part of the plots of Shakespeare's history plays and tragedies, they are most commonly depicted as failed attempts to build large social structures – especially alliances between national or imperial powers – on the uncertain basis of this smaller social unit.

In *Antony and Cleopatra*, the suggestion that the widower, Antony, should marry Caesar's sister Octavia is Agrippa's idea for preventing these two potentates from going to war with one another:

AGRIPPA
　　To hold you in perpetual amity,
　　To make you brothers, and to knit your hearts
　　With an unslipping knot …
　　　　　　　　　… By this marriage
　　All little jealousies which now seem great,

And all great fears which now import their dangers,
Would then be nothing.
(*Antony and Cleopatra*, 2.2.131–40)

Readers and theatre-goers do not need to know their Plutarch to anticipate that this is a vain hope. In Shakespeare's *Henry V*, the dynastic marriage comes at the end of the play and is immediately followed by an epilogue that reports its failure to hold the two countries under one leadership:

CHORUS
Henry the Sixth, in infant bands crowned king
Of France and England, did this king succeed,
Whose state so many had the managing
That they lost France and made his England bleed.
(*Henry V*, Epilogue 9–12)

The one play in which Shakespeare depicts the creation of a successful international union is *Cymbeline*, and it most markedly is not built on the foundations of marriage or the family. Indeed, as we saw in Chapter 2, in *Cymbeline*, marriage and the family are pointedly offered as anti-models for a happy social life.

Hierarchies and complex systems

What, then, are we to make of the way that weak and strong bonds between persons arising from the genetic pressures of family relatedness and the social pressures of cultural affinity interact to form larger social networks? The biological model of the organism can take us quite a long way in offering a series of correspondences between the organization of parts at one level and the organization of parts at another. Most clearly, the father as so-called head of the family unit in patriarchal social structures has parallels with the monarch as the head of the national social structure. What should strike us most about these two systems is that they are self-reproducing, so that biological systems are not merely analogous to these social structures: the similarity goes much deeper than that.

Karl Marx observes that what makes capitalism a long-lived and formidable system of production is that it generates in people the means of its own perpetuation; it replicates itself. The bourgeois neoclassical model of behaviour imagined that individuals are free to make decisions, that they survey their economic options and then make choices that reflect their determination of what is the best use of their time and resources. Marx shows that this is not the experience of most people. Rather, external economic forces become mirrored in individual behaviour so as to perpetuate existing economic relations. The extraction of surplus value by the capitalist necessarily results 'in reproducing the working man as a working man, and the capitalist as a capitalist'.[20] This principle of systems self-replicating by producing in human beings the need or desire to reproduce them is but one example of a wider principle of self-replication, and it directs attention away from the individual components to consider the emergent phenomena of the system.

In a brilliant analysis of the Freudian psychodynamics of the family, Nancy Chodorow argues that mothering, too, is such an emergent phenomenon:

[T]he contemporary reproduction of mothering occurs through social structurally induced psychological processes. … Women, as mothers, produce daughters with mothering capacities and the desire to mother. These capacities and needs are built into and grow out of the mother–daughter relationship itself. By contrast, women as mothers (and men as not-mothers) produce sons whose nurturant capacities and needs have been systematically curtailed and repressed.[21]

What is being described here is a complex system, the normative family unit of modern industrial capitalism, within which not only economic but also (according to Chodorow at least) psycho-sexual forces are operating to reproduce the system in the next generation.

In the study of complex systems, mid-twentieth-century researchers found striking similarities between biological systems, physical structures and social systems, including the organization of large business corporations. This made those working in the fields of zoology, information technology, business studies and cybernetics wonder whether their shared models had real significance. As the political scientist and chair of the Department of Industrial Management, Herbert A. Simon, puts it, 'systems of such diverse kinds could hardly be expected to have any nontrivial properties in common'.[22] Having lowered his audience's expectations, Simon goes on to outline some startlingly non-trivial properties that biological organisms and social systems actually do have in common regarding what he called the architecture of their complexity.

The key feature of what Simon calls complex systems is that they are 'made up of a large number of parts that interact in a nonsimple way ... the whole is more than the sum of the parts, not in an ultimate, metaphysical sense, but in the important pragmatic sense that, given the properties of the parts and the laws of their interaction, it is not a trivial matter to infer the properties of the whole', and that they are hierarchical, being 'composed of subsystems that, in turn, have their own subsystems'.[23] These conditions are met by the systems we are concerned with in biology and human social interaction, both during times of social order and, as we have seen, times of social unrest. The key facet, for Simon, is hierarchy, which he finds to be favoured by evolution. A hierarchy here means a system made up of interrelated subsystems each of which itself is a hierarchy, working downwards until we reach some lowest level where we find whatever we choose (arbitrarily) to call unitary elements. In societies, the lowest level is typically the citizen, or subject; in organisms, it is the cell.

Hierarchies have different degrees of flatness in the sense of how many subsystems lie underneath each system: the more subsystems per system, the flatter the hierarchy. (At the limit, an utterly flat hierarchy is scarcely worth considering as a hierarchy at all.) The frontispiece by Abraham Bosse that accompanies Thomas Hobbes' landmark work of political economy, *Leviathan* (1651), shows a particularly flat hierarchy. The sovereign in this picture is composed of his people – articulating Hobbes' point about sovereignty – but the people are not differentiated and do not form smaller subsystems. There are no visible classes, trades or families in Bosse's etching, and to that extent the sovereign could just as well be Christ as an English monarch, since the principal radical innovation of Christianity from its inception was the idea that all souls are equally important and undifferentiated before God.

Systems that are what Simon calls 'decomposable' can be readily understood by considering the actions of their parts, and if they are hierarchies these parts interact only in the vertical dimension. In business organization, this would be the extreme case, where each employee responds to instructions from her line manager and issues instructions to her subordinates but is never affected in her judgements by her peers. This of course would be most unusual. Most hierarchies are what Simon calls 'nearly decomposable', in that vertical forces are much stronger than horizontal forces, but the latter are not entirely absent; and the forces holding a subsystem together are stronger than forces operating between subsystems but the latter, again, are not entirely absent. The behaviour of such systems is, because of these additional interactions, complex rather than simple, but is not chaotic.

If we apply this model to the characters in Shakespeare's history plays the analogies are readily apparent. The tightly bound family unit is a subsystem of the larger social structure, but the internal family bonds ought ordinarily to be much stronger than the bonds of loyalty to the monarch. In *Richard II*, the Duke of York finds that his son, Aumerle, has plotted to kill the new king, Henry IV, to whom York races to denounce his son. At the moment of discovery, the Duchess had tried to persuade her husband to conceal the plot, invoking the biological imperative: 'Have we more sons? Or are we like to have? / Is not my teeming date drunk up with time? … Is he not like thee? Is he not thine own?' (*Richard II*, 5.2.90–4). York is unmoved.

His mother's rhetoric failing, Aumerle hastens to the king to seek a pardon and just as he is about to get it he is interrupted by the entrance of his father the duke demanding rigorous punishment. Henry IV finds a way to reinterpret the biological relation in order to grant Aumerle's request for pardon:

KING HENRY
    O loyal father of a treacherous son!
    Thou sheer, immaculate, and silver fountain,
    From whence this stream through muddy passages
    Hath held his current and defiled himself,
    Thy overflow of good converts to bad,
    And thy abundant goodness shall excuse
    This deadly blot in thy digressing son.
    (*Richard II*, 5.3.58–64)

This is a reversal of the principle that the sins of the father are inherited by the son, which appears in several books of the Bible, and is mentioned in the Commandment against worshipping graven images (Exod. 20.5).

Paradoxically, Henry IV uses York's extreme loyalty in what we would call the vertical direction (up to the monarch) and absence of a horizontal loyalty (to his own son) against him. That is, Henry uses the vertical loyalty as a justification for granting what the duke would be asking for – the pardon – if his loyalty were primarily horizontal, if he cared more for his son than his king. York sees that such inverted logic is self-defeating and that to privilege the vertical relationship the horizontal truly has to be disavowed:

YORK
>So shall my virtue be his vice's bawd,
>And he shall spend mine honour with his shame,
>As thriftless sons their scraping fathers' gold.
>Mine honour lives when his dishonour dies,
>Or my shamed life in his dishonour lies.
>Thou kill'st me in his life: giving him breath
>The traitor lives, the true man's put to death.
>(*Richard II*, 5.3.65–71)

Logical as York's answer is, the effect upon an audience is bound to be that he loses sympathy. At a deep biological level we disapprove of favouring a vertical, chosen, social bond over a genetic one.

Writing as the basis of social networks

Shakespeare develops further this theme of competing social networks – biological and political – in his next two history plays. In *Richard II*, the conspiracy is recorded in a set of six documents that all the conspirators sign, called by Peter Ure an 'indenture sextipartite'.[24] This means that, if any one of them is captured while in possession of this document, all are incriminated. In *Henry IV, Part 1*, the instigators of another anti-Lancastrian conspiracy against the same king also have indentures drawn up, but as far as we can tell these remain with Owen Glendŵr in Wales (*Henry IV, Part I*, 3.1.255–61). The documents we do repeatedly see in connection with the conspiracy are letters passing between its members, which is explicitly the plan from the outset: 'No further go in this,' says Worcester to Hotspur, 'Than I by letters shall direct your course' (*Henry IV, Part I*, 1.3.286–7).

Although many must pass that are not shown, what we see Hotspur getting are disappointing letters, such as the one from an unnamed conspirator that he enters reading at the start of 2.4, and then, more seriously, the one by which his father Northumberland insincerely excuses himself from the coming battle on the grounds of illness (*Henry IV, Part I*, 4.1.12–31). Like York in *Richard II*, Northumberland in *Henry IV, Part I* behaves unnaturally in not putting his son beyond all other considerations, although just why he feigns illness to avoid supporting his son is never made plain to the audience.

The whole conspiracy runs on letters:

HOTSPUR
> Is there not my father, my uncle, and myself? Lord Edmund Mortimer, my lord of York, and Owain Glyndŵr? Is there not besides the Douglas? Have I not all their letters, to meet me in arms by the ninth of the next month?
> (*Henry IV, Part 1*, 2.4.22–6)

This was something new for Shakespeare's history plays, as his preceding history plays (most notably the Henry VI cycle) scarcely mentioned letters at all. If we put Shakespeare's plays in order of how frequently letters are mentioned in dialogue or stage directions, comedies dominate the top of the list, with *The Two Gentlemen of Verona* (46 times), *Love's Labour's Lost* (38 times), *The Merry Wives of Windsor* (35 times), *All's Well that Ends Well* (30 times), *Twelfth Night* (27 times) and *The Merchant of Venice* (24 times) all having more letters than *Henry IV, Parts I and II* (13 and 17 times respectively); and the Henry VI cycle has fewer still (10, 2 and 6 times respectively). In other words, towards the end of the 1590s, as part of his introduction of comedy into the second tetralogy (it being almost entirely absent from the first tetralogy), Shakespeare brought in his well-honed dramaturgy of letter sending and receiving.

Why the sudden interest in letters? The answer seems to be that in the sending of letters one man's mind can be broadcast to several people at once. In *Henry IV, Part I,* Shakespeare twice depicts the sending of letters, and on both occasions it is this one-to-many aspect that is emphasized:

PRINCE HARRY (*giving letters*)
  Go bear this letter to Lord John of Lancaster,
  To my brother John; this to my lord of Westmorland.
  Exit Russell
  (*Henry IV, Part I*, 3.3.197–8)

ARCHBISHOP (*giving letters*)
  Hie, good Sir Michael, bear this sealèd brief
  With wingèd haste to the Lord Marshal,
  This to my cousin Scrope, and all the rest
  To whom they are directed.
  (*Henry IV, Part I*, 4.4.1–4)

The losing side, we notice, sends out more letters. As Simon points out, human communicative powers limit the social structures that can be formed: '[a person] can carry on only one conversation at a time, and although this does not limit the size of the audience to which a mass communication can be addressed, it does limit the number of people simultaneously involved in most other forms of social interaction'.[25] Simon goes on to remark 'One cannot … enact the role of "friend" with large numbers of other people'; this will become relevant when we turn to the latest kinds of social network.

In observing that the first tetralogy of Shakespeare's history plays did not employ comedy and did not use letters, it might be objected that I have overlooked the grimly comic Jack Cade rebellion in *Henry VI, Part II*. Certainly Cade has a strong view about the social function of written language and especially its manifestation in ink and parchment:

CADE
  Is not this a lamentable thing that of the skin of
  an innocent lamb should be made parchment? That
  parchment, being scribbled

o'er, should undo a man? Some say the bee stings, but I
say 'tis the bee's wax. For I did but seal once to a thing,
and I was never mine own man since.
(*Henry VI, Part II*, 4.2.84)

Once he has Lord Saye in his power, Cade finds an even more
serious charge to lay against him:

CADE
whereas before, our forefathers had no other books but
the score and the tally, thou hast caused printing to be
used and, contrary to the King his crown and dignity,
thou hast built a paper-mill.
(*Henry VI, Part II*, 4.7.32–5)

Social structures created by language were spatially organized
until the invention of writing, since they required the presence
of listeners within earshot of the speaker. With the invention
of printing, of course, such structures could be created across
vast geographical spans and could involve large numbers
of people. Until the invention of the twentieth-century
electronic media, printing was the epitome of one-to-many
communication.

Overall, Shakespeare refers to books far less often than
to letters: 157 occurrences across the canon against 470. In
respect of powerful social communication, his really strong
contrast was between oratory and writing, the former most
expertly practised by Antony in *Julius Caesar* to raise a mob,
and by More in *Sir Thomas More* to quell one. We might
easily explain this by saying that Shakespeare was writing
about largely illiterate groups and writing for a largely
illiterate theatre audience. But the second half of this explanation can no longer stand. In the past ten years it has been
discovered that Shakespeare had ambitions to be a literary
writer as well as a theatre writer. That is, he cared about the
print publication of his plays and he wrote with his readership
in mind.[26] Moreover, not only did Shakespeare have ambitions

to be a successful writer in print but he also succeeded in them: he actually was by far the most widely sold dramatist of his age.[27]

When considering Shakespeare's crowd scenes and what they tell us about the construction of social networks in his time, the notion of a hierarchy's flatness turns out to be surprisingly useful. Although Dick the Butcher just about qualifies as Jack Cade's side-kick, the hierarchy depicted in the mob of *Henry VI, Part II* is essentially flat: the crowd has no discernible structure. The rebels in *Sir Thomas More* are rather more clearly led by a collective comprising John Lincoln, Doll Williamson, her husband Williamson and the Betts brothers. That they have names is itself an index of their importance: mob members are usually nameless.

As argued above, the crowd of citizens at the start of *Coriolanus* share this characteristic of being personalized and differentiated, especially if editors retain the first edition's speech prefixes. With the introduction of the Tribunes as a new social role, the social organization of Rome's people becomes markedly more stratified and hierarchical, and the play strongly suggests that this is not the democratic development we might easily take it to be. The case of Jack Cade's rebellion might seem to be the anomaly here, being by far the most unreasonable and unthinkable kind of collective action, serving the vanity of one man. If so, we can, if we wish to absolve Shakespeare of this crudity, take comfort in the mounting evidence that this part of the play was not, in fact, written by Shakespeare but by his co-author, probably Christopher Marlowe.[28]

With our new view of Shakespeare the would-be and actual literary dramatist, we can revisit the importance of books within his plays. As we have seen in the counts of their occurrence, they are not as ubiquitous as letters, and few actual books appear on stage. In *Titus Andronicus* a copy of Ovid's *Metamorphoses* enables the muted Lavinia to begin to convey what has happened to her (4.1.30–57), and in *King Lear* Edmund pretends to read from a book of astronomical predictions (*King Lear*, 1.2.140–1). In *Hamlet*, Ophelia and Hamlet both pretend to read from books (2.2 and 3.1), and in *Richard III*, pretending to be absorbed in a religious book is one of the feigned 'ornaments to know a holy man' (3.7.99).

There is something recurrently uncanny regarding books in Shakespeare's plays even when their readers are innocent. Brutus loses but finds again a book and looks for his place: 'Let me see, let me see; is not the leaf turn'd down Where I left reading? Here it is, I think.' As soon as he recovers his place there occurs the stage direction '*Enter the Ghost of Caesar*' (*Julius Caesar*, 4.2.325). Brutus first notices the ghost because his candle reacts to it: 'How ill this taper burns!' (*Julius Caesar*, 4.2.326). In a parallel scene, Imogen also turns down the page to mark her place, also has a taper burning as she reads, and is likewise uncannily visited. But, according to Iachimo, the candle reacts not to his presence but to hers: 'The flame o' th' taper / Bows toward her, and would underpeep her lids' (*Cymbeline*, 2.2.19–20). Looking closely at the turned-down page, Iachimo finds what she has been reading, and again it is Ovid's *Metamorphoses* (*Cymbeline*, 4.2.44–6).

Yet, strangely, this recurrent interest in the uncanny nature of books is not Shakespeare's main interest in them, for books are most often mentioned in his plays in analogies with the human body, especially the face. The first occurrence is in Shakespeare's early narrative poem *The Rape of Lucrece*: 'Poor women's faces are their own faults' books' (line 1253). The idea is that faces can be read like books. Lady Macbeth says: 'Your face, my thane, is as a book where men / May read strange matters' (*Macbeth*, 1.5.61–2). Capulet's Wife tries to win Juliet's approbation for the man she is meant to marry with: 'Read o'er the volume of young Paris' face, / And find delight writ there with beauty's pen', taking the metaphor so far as to suggest that 'what obscured in this fair volume lies / Find written in the margin of his eyes' (*Romeo and Juliet*, 1.3.83–8). No wonder, the, that the first time she has her face pressed against her future husband's, this image returns to Juliet: 'You kiss by th' book' (*Romeo and Juliet*, 1.5.109).

Andrew Gurr observes that the bottle of liquor in *The Tempest* would be made of leather and look much like a book; hence it is much kissed, sworn upon and provides an alternative locus of authority to Prospero's differently transformative books.[29]

As we saw, Northumberland fails to support his son Hotspur in the rebellion against the new king in *Henry IV, Part I*, and at the start of the sequel he reads news of the fatal consequence of this failure in the aspect of a messenger bringing news of the battle: 'Yea, this man's brow, like to a title leaf, / Foretells the nature of a tragic volume' (*Henry IV, Part II*, 1.1.60–1). This second tetralogy begins with the most drawn-out version of the face-as-book metaphor. In the first of the plays, Richard II is usurped by Bolingbroke (who becomes Henry IV) and is required to read to Parliament a statement of his wrongdoing lest the commons remain unsatisfied that he was rightfully deposed:

> RICHARD
> They shall be satisfied. I'll read enough
> When I do see the very book indeed
> Where all my sins are writ, and that's myself.
> *Enter one with a glass*
> (*Richard II*, 4.1.263–5)

Richard is amazed to find that his experiences are not written on his face: 'No deeper wrinkles yet?' (*Richard II*, 4.1.267). Othello, likewise, thinks of experiences as being written on the face. Staring at Desdemona's face he asks: 'Was this fair paper, this most goodly book, / Made to write "whore" upon?' (*Othello*, 4.2.73–4).

Why does Shakespeare so strongly associate books with faces and so little with communities of readers? As we saw at the end of Chapter 2, Shakespeare commonly connected the process of printing with the processes of sexual reproduction and coining, the mechanical stamping out of a copy. Faces are the most visibly distinctive and individuating parts of human beings – headless Cloten is indistinguishable from

Posthumus – and, as Shakespeare repeatedly dramatizes, they are a synthesis of what we would call genetic inheritance (since children's faces look like those of their parents) and of experiences, which are written onto faces and read from them. They exemplify the Nature/Nurture relationship.

Shakespeare had little opportunity to see the communities of readers that were formed by mass publication, beyond the few that would frequent the bookshops of St Paul's Churchyard, as he did. At the start of his career, play publication was essentially an anonymous activity, with the genre and the theatre company being stated on attention-attracting title-pages, but not the author. During his lifetime this changed, but Shakespeare was essentially too early to see in print the great explosion of what we now call English Literature. Erne lists the first known collectors of volumes of Shakespeare and other early modern dramatists, and although this exercise usefully dispels the idea that no one was serious about this material until the eighteenth century it is noticeable that the collections start to become significant at the end of and shortly after Shakespeare's career, not at the height of it.[30] Shakespeare would have known that he was selling well, but a community of his readers had scarcely begun to form before he retired.

This may not be the whole explanation for Shakespeare's depiction of letters rather than books as the means for organizing concerted activity. Letters are bidirectional communication calling for an answer from the recipient, whereas books are essential, unidirectional communication. In an age when many more people could read than write, and many more could write than could ever hope to become a published author, a book could be consumed by many more people than could ever hope to answer it with a book of their own. Although communities of published authors certainly sprang up in Europe from the seventeenth to the twentieth centuries in far greater numbers than could possibly have been sustained by medieval scribal publication, it was not until the late twentieth century that the means for many-to-many communication became widely available to most of the inhabitants of Earth.

Conclusion

Thinking about crowds and social networks in terms of biological multi-cellularity helps us to consider just what it is to be an individual and to be part of a larger grouping with shared interests. Ecocritical theory and practice require us to think in genuinely global terms about shared interests, and this turns out to be most difficult to do. It is hard for those in Bangladesh whose coastal towns are likely to be flooded in the next twenty years to make common cause with the Chinese and American consumers whose atmospheric carbon dioxide pollution will contribute to this calamity, and vice versa. But it is getting easier to do so.

Global communication

The Internet, and in particular the Worldwide Web, is the ultimate community created by reading and writing. Although it is not clear exactly how extensive a role the Internet played in recent political events such as the Arab Spring of 2010–12, the fact that repressive regimes routinely cut off Internet access to their populations in times of crisis is testimony to the widespread belief that unfettered many-to-many communication empowers ordinary citizens. The Internet is available to over three billion people – about half the world's total population – and enables the perfect and almost instantaneous copying of digital files representing writing, pictures, sounds and moving video. Within that total community there is considerable stratification by particular cultural and political interests. Although the record for most viewings of one music video is over two billion – currently held by *Gangnam Style* performed by the South Korean musician, Psy – the Internet is far more significant for its enabling of vast numbers of smaller special interest groups to overcome the limitations of geography and communicate freely.

The Internet connects people but only indirectly, since it essentially connects computers. There are two substrates for communication that the Internet thus creates: the human beings using the computers and the computers themselves. When Richard Dawkins coined the term meme for cultural replicators, he observed: 'Whenever conditions arise in which a new kind of replicator can make copies of itself, the new replicators will tend to take over, and start a new kind of evolution of their own.'[1] This seemed rather far-fetched when first stated so baldly in 1977, but the Internet has proved it to be true. Over 90 per cent of all email traffic is computer-generated advertising – so-called spam – rather than human communication. Millions of Internet-connected computers are infected with viruses that enable them to be corralled into vast networks of virtual agents – so-called bot-nets – that can be directed by those who created the viruses and used to disrupt part of the Internet for criminal or political ends.

When Tim Berners-Lee invented the Worldwide Web as a new service on the Internet he intended it to be a many-to-many communication system. That is, he expected users to create and update their own websites as frequently as they consumed the content on others' websites. This ambition went largely unrealized in the first decade of the Worldwide Web, primarily because the technical skills and online resources needed to create and update websites are considerably greater than the skills and resources needed merely to consume the content on existing websites. On the Worldwide Web, as with books in Shakespeare's time, many more people can read than write. The early web was, for this reason, essentially a one-to-many communication system that was dominated by large commercial publishers of information.

From the early 2000s this changed when several online service providers invented the means to enable individuals to create websites without extensive technical skills and offered the hosting of these sites without charge in return for the right to direct advertising at their users. This has had the beneficial effect of encouraging many more people to create their own websites, but entails the disadvantage that these are not pure Worldwide Web sites as envisaged by Berners-Lee. Rather, the new sites are merely profiles within a so-called 'walled garden' curated by large technology companies, the most successful of which is Facebook. The disadvantages of this effective privatization of the Worldwide Web are well documented, and include subjection to censorship at the whim of a private corporation and the sale of users' personal details to advertisers.

It remains to be seen whether the free Web can remain free despite users' widespread adoption of private services such as Facebook. In the reporting of political events across the world, the services called YouTube (owned by Google) and Twitter (owned by Facebook), together with the widespread ownership of small video cameras built into mobile telephones, have made it increasingly difficult for repressive regimes entirely to conceal their wrongdoing. Where political activism is itself criminalized, as in China and much of the Middle East, the technical ability to encrypt communications has kept activists safe from their governments, but, as is widely lamented, the same technologies are available to criminals and terrorists, within and outside governments.

These technical aspects of global communication are central to ecological activism in the modern world. Citizens in European countries that have yet to license widespread extraction of subterranean shale gas by the process of hydraulic fracturing (or fracking) are able to watch online video accounts of the experiences of Pennsylvanians living above the Marcellus Formation, which is being extensively mined for this hydrocarbon resource. Those who would help the Ogoni people of Nigeria resist the destruction of their land

and the killing of their people by the oil company Royal Dutch Shell are able, because of the Internet, to witness the struggle at close quarters and collectively to organize against it. The examples of how communications technology has enabled green activism may be multiplied many times.

The positive social and political benefits of information technology must not, however, blind us to its harmful aspects, including the near-slavery conditions of electronics factories in China and the centralization of personal data on computers not under the control of the persons the data concerns. Ironically, just as small devices capable of storing vast quantities of personal data have become extremely inexpensive, the information industry has succeeded in persuading many of its customers to instead store their information in something that is euphemistically called The Cloud. The connotations of ubiquity, freedom and environmentalism invoked by the term The Cloud are intended to conceal what is really meant, which is that users are storing their personal information on someone else's computer to which they have access only by way of the Internet and over which they have little direct control if things go wrong or if governments demand to inspect it. Moreover, far from being green, the warehouses containing the servers for The Cloud consume vast quantities of electrical energy, almost all of which is made by burning fossil fuels.

Entropy, Shakespeare and green politics

The atmospheric gases of the Earth are in a state of extreme disequilibrium, and if they were not the planet would be sure to contain no life. Oxygen and methane exist in our atmosphere in quantities that would be impossible were they not endlessly renewed by the life-forms on Earth, since left to itself methane readily combusts in the presence of oxygen. James Lovelock's Gaia hypothesis insists that this atmospheric disequilibrium is not a happy coincidence but is itself the product of life existing on Earth. Humankind's addition of large quantities of carbon dioxide to the atmosphere since the Industrial Revolution of the late eighteenth century does not threaten the continued existence of life on Earth, only the continued flourishing of human life.

By raising the atmosphere's capacity to retain the energy of the Sun's electromagnetic radiation falling on the Earth, atmospheric carbon dioxide and other greenhouse gases are expected, according to the Intergovernmental Panel on Climate Change's Fifth Report of 2014, to raise the average temperature on Earth by more than 2° Celsius by the year 2100, with the rise continuing thereafter. The Panel's remit does not cover speculation about the social or political consequences of such a temperature rise, and the report is confined instead to certainties about the changing patterns of global weather, including the location and intensities of monsoons, and the rising sea levels. All responsible scientific speculations about a rise of 2° Celsius, or more, predict catastrophic collapse of food production in large parts of the world and mass flooding in areas hitherto considered relatively unaffected, including the continental United States.

One way to think about the transfer of energy from the Sun to the Earth and the processes of life is in terms of the concept of entropy, meaning the amount of unusable energy in a system. Life-forms by definition represent local lowering of the entropy in an environment: they turn the materials around them into complex ordering of matter, and create centres of usable energy. Photosynthesis is an archetypal instance of this process. In order to conserve the total energy involved – as the Second Law of Thermodynamics requires – we have to account for the local lowering of entropy represented by a tree's growing in one's garden by offsetting it against the corresponding increase in entropy on the surface of the Sun as a small amount of hydrogen is converted into helium to generate the radiation (sunlight) that the tree subsequently captures and exploits.

Over half a century ago, C. P. Snow equated ignorance of the Second Law of Thermodynamics to ignorance of the works of Shakespeare, and deplored humanists' lack of basic knowledge in science.[2] According to Snow, the inability of the two cultures of the sciences and humanities to communicate was an obstacle to the common understanding of modern life. The criticism remains true in the early twenty-first century, and the consequences of widespread scientific illiteracy are even more dangerous for the future of human civilization. In order to understand the debates, ecocritics need to understand the technical language in which Earth Systems Science is conducted, and those who wish to be ecocritical of Shakespeare should heed Snow's warning that making sense of the Second Law of Thermodynamics is as important as making sense of the plays.

There are aspects of the notion of entropy that apply as well to language construction as they do to the energy levels of gases and the transfer of energy from the Sun to the Earth. The details of this shared domain fall beyond the remit of the present study but are well covered in James Gleick's popularization *The Information*.[3] In thinking about orderliness in language in relation to artistic creativity, a commonly performed, indeed hackneyed, thought-experiment is to imagine a number of monkeys randomly hitting the keys of typewriters and to calculate the likelihood that one of them might type the First Folio collection of Shakespeare's plays. The standard conclusion is that undirected random key-striking would not produce even one sentence of Shakespeare during the entire lifetime of the present universe.

And yet monkeys are evolved creatures and as such they are local depressions in the entropy of the universe. Darwinian evolution itself should teach us that processes that are random can of themselves generate remarkable orderliness. Ecocritics thinking about these matters in relation to the Earth's impending escalation in surface temperature will doubtless reflect upon the environmental disorder in the weather that will accompany it. They may, too, want to imagine one of these hypothetical monkeys achieving the relatively small success that would be the typing of even just the first line of Shakespeare's first play, *The Tempest*, in the First Folio. That line would itself reflect what is going to become an increasingly common experience for many of Earth's inhabitants: '*A tempestuous noise of Thunder and Lightning heard.*'[4]

NOTES

Introduction

1   Gabriel Egan, *Shakespeare and Marx*, Oxford Shakespeare
    Topics (Oxford: Oxford University Press, 2004).

2   Harold Bloom, *The Western Canon: The Books and School of
    the Ages* (New York: Harcourt Brace, 1994), 15–41.

3   Raymond Tallis, *In Defence of Realism* (London: Edward
    Arnold, 1988); Raymond Tallis, *Not Saussure: A Critique of
    Post-Saussurean Literary Theory* (Basingstoke: Macmillan,
    1988); Raymond Tallis, *Theorrhoea and After* (Basingstoke:
    Macmillan, 1998).

4   Brian Vickers, *Appropriating Shakespeare: Contemporary
    Critical Quarrels* (New Haven, CT: Yale University Press,
    1993).

5   Terry Eagleton, *Literary Theory: An Introduction* (Oxford:
    Basil Blackwell, 1983), vii.

6   Terry Eagleton, *Ideology: An Introduction* (London: Verso,
    1991), 1–31.

7   E. M. W. Tillyard, *Shakespeare's History Plays* (London:
    Chatto and Windus, 1944).

8   J. P. Brockbank, 'The Frame of Disorder: *Henry VI*', in *Early
    Shakespeare*, eds. John Russell Brown and Bernard Harris,
    Stratford-on-Avon Studies 3 (London: Edward Arnold, 1961),
    73–99.

9   Andrew Hadfield, *Shakespeare and Republicanism* (Cambridge:
    Cambridge University Press, 2005).

10 Gabriel Egan, *Green Shakespeare: From Ecopolitics to*

Ecocriticism, Accents on Shakespeare (London: Routledge, 2006), 148–71.

11 Walter Benjamin, *Illuminations*, ed. Hannah Arendt. Trans. Harry Zohn (London: Fontana, 1992), 249.

12 John Huston, *The African Queen*, Motion Picture. Romulus Films/Horizon Pictures, 1951.

13 Egan, *Shakespeare and Marx*, 55–68.

14 Daniel C. Dennett, *The Intentional Stance* (Cambridge, MA: MIT Press, 1987).

15 Peter Singer, 'Animal Liberation': Review of Stanley Godlovitch, Rosalind Godlovitch, and John Harris, eds., *Animals, Men and Morals* (New York: Taplinger, 1971), *New York Review of Books*, 20.3 (1973): 17–21; Frans B. M. De Waal, *Chimpanzee Politics: Power and Sex Among Apes* (London: Cape, 1982); Frans B. M. De Waal, *The Ape and the Sushi Master: Cultural Reflections By a Primatologist* (London: Allen Lane, 2001).

16 Barry Commoner, *The Closing Circle: Confronting the Environmental Crisis* (New York: Knopf, 1971).

17 Clifford Geertz, *The Interpretation of Cultures* (New York: Basic Books, 1973).

18 Robert Darnton, *The Great Cat Massacre and Other Episodes in French Cultural History* (Harmondsworth: Penguin, 1985).

19 Egan, *Shakespeare and Marx*, 71–7.

Chapter 1

1 Egan, *Green Shakespeare: From Ecopolitics to Ecocriticism*, 17–50.

2 Herbert Butterfield, *The Whig Interpretation of History* (London: G. Bell, 1931).

3 Terence Hawkes, *Shakespeare in the Present*, Accents on Shakespeare (London: Routledge, 2002).

4 Hugh Grady and Terence Hawkes, eds., *Presentist*

Shakespeares, Accents on Shakespeare (London: Routledge, 2007).

5   Evelyn Gajowski, ed., *Presentism, Gender, and Sexuality in Shakespeare* (Basingstoke: Palgrave Macmillan, 2008).

6   Stephen Greenblatt, *Renaissance Self-Fashioning: From More to Shakespeare* (Chicago, IL: University of Chicago Press, 1980).

7   Cheryll Glotfelty, 'Introduction: Literary Studies in an Age of Environmental Crisis', in *The Ecocriticism Reader: Landmarks in Literary Ecology*, eds. Cheryll Glotfelty and Harold Fromm (Athens, GA: University of Georgia Press, 1996), xv–xxxvii (xviii–xix).

8   Alwin Fill, 'Ecolinguistics: The State of the Art, 1998', in *The Ecolinguistics Reader: Language, Ecology and Environment*, eds. Alwin Fill and Peter Mühlhäusler (London: Continuum, 2001), 43–53 (47).

9   Val Plumwood, *Feminism and the Mastery of Nature*, Feminism for Today (London: Routledge, 1993).

10   Plumwood, *Feminism and the Mastery of Nature*, 43.

11   Plumwood, *Feminism and the Mastery of Nature*, 47.

12   Plumwood, *Feminism and the Mastery of Nature*, 56.

13   Plumwood, *Feminism and the Mastery of Nature*, 57.

14   Robert N. Watson, *Back to Nature: The Green and the Real in the Late Renaissance* (Philadelphia: University of Pennsylvania Press, 2006).

15   Raymond Williams, *The Country and the City* (London: Chatto and Windus, 1973).

16   Jonathan Bate, *The Song of the Earth* (London: Picador, 2000).

17   Jonathan Bate, 'Shakespeare's Foolosophy', in *Shakespeare Performed: Essays in Honor of R. A. Foakes*, ed. Grace Ioppolo (Newark: University of Delaware Press, 2000), 17–32.

18   Diane Kelsey McColley, *Poetry and Ecology in the Age of Milton and Marvell*, Literary and Scientific Cultures of Early Modernity (Aldershot: Ashgate, 2007).

19   McColley, *Poetry and Ecology in the Age of Milton and Marvell*, 2.

20 McColley, *Poetry and Ecology in the Age of Milton and Marvell*, 209.

21 McColley, *Poetry and Ecology in the Age of Milton and Marvell*, 209–10.

22 McColley, *Poetry and Ecology in the Age of Milton and Marvell*, 210.

23 McColley, *Poetry and Ecology in the Age of Milton and Marvell*, 228.

24 Georgia Brown, 'Defining Nature Through Monstrosity in *Othello* and *Macbeth*', in *Early Modern Ecostudies: From the Florentine Codex to Shakespeare*, eds. Thomas Hallock, Ivo Kamps and Karen L. Raber, Early Modern Cultural Studies (New York: Palgrave Macmillan, 2008), 55–76.

25 Robert Markley, 'Summer's Lease: Shakespeare in the Little Ice Age', in *Early Modern Ecostudies: From the Florentine Codex to Shakespeare*, eds. Thomas Hallock, Ivo Kamps and Karen L. Raber, Early Modern Cultural Studies (New York: Palgrave Macmillan, 2008), 131–42 (135).

26 Sharon O'Dair, 'Slow Shakespeare: An Eco-critique of "Method" in Early Modern Literary Studies', in *Early Modern Ecostudies: From the Florentine Codex to Shakespeare*, eds. Thomas Hallock, Ivo Kamps and Karen L. Raber, Early Modern Cultural Studies (New York: Palgrave Macmillan, 2008), 11–30.

27 Jeffrey S. Theis, *Writing the Forest in Early Modern England: A Sylvan Pastoral Nation*, Medieval and Renaissance Literary Studies (Pittsburgh, PA: Duquesne University Press, 2009).

28 Theis, *Writing the Forest in Early Modern England: A Sylvan Pastoral Nation*, 302 n.12.

29 Bruce R. Smith, *The Key of Green: Passion and Perception in Renaissance Culture* (Chicago, IL: University of Chicago Press, 2009), 261 n.22.

30 Downing Cless, *Ecology and Environment in European Drama*, Advances in Theatre and Performance Studies, 14 (New York: Routledge, 2010), 91–118.

31 Cless, *Ecology and Environment in European Drama*, 98.

32 Cless, *Ecology and Environment in European Drama*, 102.

33 Cless, *Ecology and Environment in European Drama*, 117.

34 Todd A. Borlik, *Ecocriticism and Early Modern English Literature: Green Pastures*, Routledge Studies in Renaissance Literature and Culture 16 (New York: Routledge, 2011), 6.

35 Borlik, *Ecocriticism and Early Modern English Literature: Green Pastures*, 141–2.

36 Borlik, *Ecocriticism and Early Modern English Literature: Green Pastures*, 149–64.

37 Ken Hiltner, *What Else is Pastoral?: Renaissance Literature and the Environment* (Ithaca, NY: Cornell University Press, 2011).

38 Simon C. Estok, *Ecocriticism and Shakespeare: Reading Ecophobia*, Literatures, Cultures, and Environment (New York: Palgrave Macmillan, 2011).

39 Estok, *Ecocriticism and Shakespeare: Reading Ecophobia*, 128 n.2.

40 Estok, *Ecocriticism and Shakespeare: Reading Ecophobia*, 128 n.5.

41 Estok, *Ecocriticism and Shakespeare: Reading Ecophobia*, 4.

42 Estok, *Ecocriticism and Shakespeare: Reading Ecophobia*, 22, 29, 30.

43 Estok, *Ecocriticism and Shakespeare: Reading Ecophobia*, 43.

44 Vin Nardizzi, 'Shakespeare's Globe and England's Woods', *Shakespeare Studies*, 39 (2011): 54–63.

45 John Ronayne, 'Totus Mundus Agit Histrionem [The Whole World Moves the Actor]: The Interior Decorative Scheme of the Bankside Globe', in *Shakespeare's Globe Rebuilt*, eds. J. R. Mulryne, Margaret Shewring and Andrew Gurr (Cambridge: Cambridge University Press, 1997), 121–46; Siobhan Keenan and Peter Davidson, 'The Iconography of the Globe', in *Shakespeare's Globe Rebuilt*, eds. J. R. Mulryne, Margaret Shewring and Andrew Gurr (Cambridge: Cambridge University Press, 1997), 147–56.

46 Sharon O'Dair, '"To Fright the Animals and to Kill Them Up": Shakespeare and Ecology', *Shakespeare Studies*, 39 (2011): 74–83 (80).

47 Steve Mentz, 'Shakespeare's Beach House, or the Green and

the Blue in *Macbeth*', *Shakespeare Studies*, 39 (2011): 84–93 (91).

48   Mentz, 'Shakespeare's Beach House, or the Green and the Blue in *Macbeth*' (92).

49   Dan Brayton, *Shakespeare's Ocean: An Ecocritical Exploration*, Under the Sign of Nature: Explorations in Ecocriticism (Charlottesville, VA: University of Virginia Press, 2012), 18, 37.

50   James Lovelock, *The Revenge of Gaia: Why the Earth is Fighting Back and How we Can Still Save Humanity* (London: Penguin, 2006), 37.

51   Evelyn Tribble and John Sutton, 'Cognitive Ecology as a Framework for Shakespearean Studies', *Shakespeare Studies*, 39 (2011): 94–103.

52   Evelyn Tribble, 'Distributing Cognition in the Globe', *Shakespeare Quarterly*, 56 (2005): 135–55; Evelyn Tribble, *Cognition in the Globe: Attention and Memory in Shakespeare's Theatre*, Cognitive Studies in Literature and Performance (Basingstoke: Palgrave Macmillan, 2011).

53   Rebecca Laroche, 'Ophelia's Plants and the Death of Violets', in *Ecocritical Shakespeare*, eds. Lynne Bruckner and Dan Brayton, Literary and Scientific Cultures of Early Modernity (Aldershot: Ashgate, 2011), 211–21.

54   Franco Zeffirelli, *Hamlet*, Motion Picture. Warner/Le Studio Canal+/Carolco/Icon/Marquis/Nelson, 1990; Kenneth Branagh, *Hamlet*, Motion Picture. Turner/Castle Rock/Columbia/Fishmonger, 1996.

55   Peter Holland, 'Feasting and Starving: Staging Food in Shakespeare', *Shakespeare Jahrbuch*, 145 (2009): 11–28 (11).

56   Jennifer Waldron, 'Of Stones and Stony Hearts: Desdemona, Hermione, and Post-Reformation Theatre', in *The Indistinct Human in Renaissance Literature*, eds. Jean E. Feerick and Vin Nardizzi, Early Modern Cultural Studies (New York: Palgrave Macmillan, 2012), 205–27.

57   Waldron, 'Of Stones and Stony Hearts: Desdemona, Hermione, and Post-Reformation Theatre' (213).

58   Bruce Boehrer, *Environmental Degradation in Jacobean Drama* (Cambridge: Cambridge University Press, 2013).

59 Boehrer, *Environmental Degradation in Jacobean Drama*, 46.

60 Boehrer, *Environmental Degradation in Jacobean Drama*, 77.

61 Leah Knight, *Reading Green in Early Modern England* (Burlington, VT: Ashgate, 2013).

62 Egan, *Green Shakespeare: From Ecopolitics to Ecocriticism*.

63 James E. Lovelock, 'Reflections on Gaia', in *Scientists Debate Gaia: The Next Century*, eds. Stephen H. Schneider, James R. Miller, Eileen Crist and Penelope J. Boston (Cambridge, MA: Massachusetts Institute of Technology Press, 2004), 1–5.

64 Daniel Dennett, 'How Has Darwin's Theory of Natural Selection Transformed Our View of Humanity's Place in the Universe?', in *Life: The Science of Biology*, eds. William K. Purves, David Sadava, Gordon H. Orians and H. Craig Heller, 7th edn (Sunderland, MA: Sinauer, 2003), II: Evolution, Diversity, and Ecology, 523.

Chapter 2

1 G. Wilson Knight, *The Crown of Life: Essays in Interpretation of Shakespeare's Final Plays* (Oxford: Oxford University Press, 1947).

2 Martin Wiggins, *Drama and the Transfer of Power in Renaissance England* (Oxford: Oxford University Press, 2012), 104–5.

3 Branagh, *Hamlet*.

4 Watson, *Back to Nature: The Green and the Real in the Late Renaissance*.

5 Jean-Baptiste Lamarck, *Zoological Philosophy: An Exposition with Regard to the Natural History of Animals*. Translated and introduced by Hugh Elliot (London: Macmillan, 1914), 113.

6 Richard Dawkins, *The Blind Watchmaker*, 2nd edn (London: Penguin, 1991), 357.

7 John Locke, *An Essay Concerning Human Understanding*, Wing L2738 (London: Elizabeth Holt for Thomas Basset, 1690), F3r.

8   Steven Pinker, *The Blank Slate: The Modern Denial of Human Nature* (London: Penguin, 2002), 5.

9   Pinker, *The Blank Slate: The Modern Denial of Human Nature*, 435–9.

10 W. D. Hamilton, 'The Genetical Evolution of Social Behaviour [Part] I', *Journal of Theoretical Biology*, 7 (1964): 1–16; W. D. Hamilton, 'The Genetical Evolution of Social Behaviour [Part] II', *Journal of Theoretical Biology*, 7 (1964): 17–52.

11 Richard Dawkins, *The Selfish Gene* (Oxford: Oxford University Press, 1976).

12 Richard Dawkins, *The Extended Phenotype: The Gene as the Unit of Selection* (Oxford: Oxford University Press, 1982).

13 Richard Dawkins, *The Extended Phenotype: The Long Reach of the Gene*, 2nd edn with a new foreword by Daniel Dennett (Oxford: Oxford University Press, 1999), 235–6.

14 Dawkins, *The Extended Phenotype: The Long Reach of the Gene*, 236.

15 James E. Lovelock, 'Daisy World: A Cybernetic Proof of the Gaia Hypothesis', *Coevolution Quarterly*, 38 (1983): 66–72.

16 Timothy M. Lenton, 'Gaia and Natural Selection', doi:10.1038/28792, *Nature*, 394 (1998): 439–47; Stephen H. Schneider, James R. Miller, Eileen Crist and Penelope J. Boston, eds., *Scientists Debate Gaia: The Next Century* (Cambridge, MA: Massachusetts Institute of Technology Press, 2004).

17 Nessa Carey, *The Epigenetics Revolution: How Modern Biology is Rewriting Our Understanding of Genetics, Disease and Inheritance* (London: Icon, 2011), 94.

18 Carey, *The Epigenetics Revolution: How Modern Biology is Rewriting Our Understanding of Genetics, Disease and Inheritance*, 97–114.

19 Jeffrey Masten, *Textual Intercourse: Collaboration, Authorship, and Sexualities in Renaissance Drama*, Cambridge Studies in Renaissance Literature and Culture 14 (Cambridge: Cambridge University Press, 1997), 75–93.

20 Marjorie Garber, *Shakespeare's Ghost Writers: Literature as Uncanny Causality* (London: Methuen, 1987), 1–36.

21 Masten, *Textual Intercourse: Collaboration, Authorship, and Sexualities in Renaissance Drama*, 87.

22 Masten, *Textual Intercourse: Collaboration, Authorship, and Sexualities in Renaissance Drama*, 89.

23 Masten, *Textual Intercourse: Collaboration, Authorship, and Sexualities in Renaissance Drama*, 90–3.

24 Stanley Wells, Gary Taylor, John Jowett and William Montgomery, *William Shakespeare: A Textual Companion* (Oxford: Oxford University Press, 1987), 556–92.

25 Gabriel Egan, *The Struggle for Shakespeare's Text: Twentieth-century Editorial Theory and Practice* (Cambridge: Cambridge University Press, 2010), 100–28.

26 Wendy Wall, 'De-generation: Editions, Offspring, and *Romeo and Juliet*', in *From Performance to Print in Shakespeare's England*, eds. Peter Holland and Stephen Orgel, Redefining British Theatre History 2 (Basingstoke: Palgrave Macmillan, 2006), 152–70.

27 William Shakespeare and George Wilkins, *[Pericles] The Late, and Much Admired Play Called Pericles, Prince of Tyre*, STC 22334 BEPD 284a (Q1) (London: [William White and Thomas Creede] for Henry Gosson, 1609), A2r.

28 Philip Sidney, *The Defence of Poesie*, STC 22535 (London: [Thomas Creede] for William Ponsonby, 1595), B2r.

29 Ann Thompson, *Shakespeare's Chaucer: A Study in Literary Origins*, Liverpool English Texts and Studies 16 (Liverpool: Liverpool University Press, 1978), 3–8.

30 Masten, *Textual Intercourse: Collaboration, Authorship, and Sexualities in Renaissance Drama*, 129.

31 Gary Taylor, 'Shakespeare's Midlife Crisis', *Guardian (newspaper)*, 3 May (2004): 11.

32 John Gower, *Confessio Amantis*, STC 12142 (London: William Caxton, 1493 [actually, 1483]), A2v; John Gower, *Confessio Amantis*, STC 12143 (London: Thomas Berthelette, 1532), A1r; John Gower, *Confessio Amantis*, STC 12144 (London: Thomas Berthelette, 1554), A1r.

33 MacDonald P. Jackson, *Defining Shakespeare:* Pericles *as Test Case* (Oxford: Oxford University Press, 2003).

34 William Shakespeare, *Pericles*, ed. Suzanne Gossett, The Arden Shakespeare (London: Thomson Learning, 2004), 3.0.55–7n.

35 Steve Mentz, 'Strange Weather in *King Lear*', *Shakespeare*, 6 (2010): 139–52.

36 Shakespeare & Wilkins, *[Pericles] The Late, and Much Admired Play Called Pericles, Prince of Tyre*, E2r.

37 Wells, Taylor, Jowett and Montgomery, *William Shakespeare: A Textual Companion*, 11.13n.

38 Shakespeare, *Pericles*, 3.1.35–6n.

39 Shakespeare, *Pericles*, 3.2.91–2n.

40 Martin Daly and Margo Wilson, *Homicide*, Foundations of Human Behavior (New York: Aldine de Gruyter, 1988); Martin Daly and Margo Wilson, *The Truth About Cinderella: A Darwinian View of Parental Love*, Darwinism Today (London: Weidenfeld and Nicolson, 1998).

41 Shakespeare and Wilkins, *[Pericles] The Late, and Much Admired Play Called Pericles, Prince of Tyre*, H1r.

42 Wells, Taylor, Jowett and Montgomery, *William Shakespeare: A Textual Companion*, 556–60, 19.138n.

43 William Ingram, 'The "Evolution" of the Elizabethan Playing Company', in *The Development of Shakespeare's Theater*, ed. John H. Astington, AMS Studies in the Renaissance 24 (New York: AMS, 1992), 13–28; William Ingram, *The Business of Playing: The Beginnings of the Adult Professional Theater in Elizabethan England* (Ithaca, NY: Cornell University Press, 1992), 67–91.

44 William Shakespeare, *The Winter's Tale*, ed. John Pitcher, The Arden Shakespeare (London: Methuen, 2010): 141 n.8.

45 E. M. W. Tillyard, *The Elizabethan World Picture* (London: Chatto and Windus, 1943).

46 William Shakespeare, *The Winter's Tale*, eds. Robert Kean Turner, Virginia Westling Haas, Robert A. Jones, Andrew J. Sabol, Patricia E. Tatspaugh, The New Variorum Edition of Shakespeare (New York: The Modern Language Association of America, 2005), TLN 1029–30n.

47 Hugh Quarshie, *Second Thoughts About Othello*, International
    Shakespeare Association Occasional Papers 7 (Chipping
    Campden: International Shakespeare Association, 1999), 10–11.

48 William Shakespeare, *The Works*, ed. Alexander Pope, 6 vols
    (London: Jacob Tonson, 1723), VI: *Troilus and Cressida*;
    Cymbeline; *Romeo and Juliet*; *Hamlet*; *Othello*, 119.

49 George Chapman, *The Widow's Tears*, STC 4994 BEPD 301a
    (London: [William Stansby] for John Browne, 1612), G2v;
    George Chapman, *The Widow's Tears*, ed. Akihiro Yamada,
    Revels Plays (London: Methuen, 1975), xxxi–xxxiii.

50 Gary Taylor, 'The Structure of Performance: Act-intervals in
    the London Theatres, 1576–1642', in *Shakespeare Reshaped,
    1606–1623*, eds. Gary Taylor and John Jowett, Oxford
    Shakespeare Studies (Oxford: Clarendon Press, 1993), 3–50;
    Richard Hosley, 'Was There a Music-room in Shakespeare's
    Globe?', *Shakespeare Survey*, 13 (1960): 113–23.

51 Anne Laurence, *Women in England, 1500–1760: A Social
    History* (London: Weidenfeld and Nicolson, 1994), 269.

52 William Shakespeare, *Comedies, Histories and Tragedies*, STC
    22273 (F1) (London: Isaac and William Jaggard for Edward
    Blount, John Smethwick, Isaac Jaggard and William Aspley,
    1623), aaa6r; Zachary Lesser and Peter Stallybrass, 'The First
    Literary *Hamlet* and the Commonplacing of Professional
    Plays', *Shakespeare Quarterly*, 59 (2008): 371–420.

53 Shakespeare, *Comedies, Histories and Tragedies*, bbb3v.

54 Shakespeare, *Comedies, Histories and Tragedies*, bbb6r.

55 Douglas A. Brooks, ed., *Printing and Parenting in Early
    Modern England*, Women and Gender in the Early Modern
    World (Aldershot: Ashgate, 2005); Helen Smith, '"A Man in
    Print"?: Shakespeare and the Representation of the Press', in
    Shakespeare's Book: Essays in Reading, Writing and Reception,
    eds. Richard Meek, Jane Rickard and Richard Wilson
    (Manchester: Manchester University Press, 2008), 59–78.

56 David Wootton, '"Traffic of the Mind – Facts, Theories,
    Theories of Facts": The Scientific Revolution and a Forty
    Year Struggle Not to be Confined By Yesterday's Questions',
    Review of Robert S. Westman, *The Copernican Question:*

Prognostication, Skepticism, and Celestial Order (Berkeley, CA: University of California Press, 2011), and Steven Shapin and Simon Schaffer, *Leviathan and the Air-pump: Hobbes, Boyle, and the Experimental Life*, New edn (Princeton, NJ: Princeton University Press, 2011), *Times Literary Supplement*, No. 5664 (21 October 2011): 3–5; Nick Wilding, '"The Strangest Piece of News": Review of David Wootton *Watcher of the Skies* (New Haven, CT: Yale University Press, 2010), and J. L. Heilbron, *Galileo* (Oxford: Oxford University Press, 2010)', *London Review of Books*, 33.11 (2 June 2014): 31–2.

57   Peter W. M. Blayney, *The First Folio of Shakespeare* (Washington, DC: Folger Library Publications, 1991), 7.

58   Lukas Erne, *Shakespeare as Literary Dramatist* (Cambridge: Cambridge University Press, 2003); Lukas Erne, *Shakespeare and the Book Trade* (Cambridge: Cambridge University Press, 2013).

59   E. A. J. Honigmann, 'How Happy Was Shakespeare with the Printed Versions of His Plays?', *Modern Language Review*, 105 (2010): 937–51.

Chapter 3

1   Lynn Sagan [later Margulis], 'On the Origin of Mitosing Cells', *Journal of Theoretical Biology*, 14 (1967): 225–74; Lynn Margulis, *Origin of Eukaryotic Cells* (New Haven, CT: Yale University Press, 1971).

2   Erica Fudge, *Perceiving Animals: Humans and Beasts in Early Modern English Culture* (Basingstoke: Macmillan, 2000), 1.

3   Fudge, *Perceiving Animals: Humans and Beasts in Early Modern English Culture*, 11–33.

4   Erica Fudge, *Brutal Reasoning: Animals, Rationality, and Humanity in Early Modern England* (Ithaca, NY: Cornell University Press, 2006), 147–93.

5   Bruce Boehrer, *Shakespeare Among the Animals: Nature and*

Society in the Drama of Early Modern England, Early Modern Cultural Studies (Basingstoke: Palgrave, 2002).

6 Boehrer, *Shakespeare Among the Animals: Nature and Society in the Drama of Early Modern England*, 3.

7 Bruce Boehrer, *Animal Characters: Nonhuman Beings in Early Modern Literature* (Philadelphia: University of Pennsylvania Press, 2010).

8 Laurie Shannon, *The Accommodated Animal: Cosmopolity in Shakespeare's Locales* (Chicago, IL: University of Chicago Press, 2013), 18.

9 Shannon, *The Accommodated Animal: Cosmopolity in Shakespeare's Locales*, 127–73.

10 Tillyard, *The Elizabethan World Picture*; Gabriel Egan, 'Gaia and the Great Chain of Being', in *Ecocritical Shakespeare*, eds. Lynne Bruckner and Daniel Brayton, Literary and Scientific Cultures of Early Modernity (Aldershot: Ashgate, 2011), 57–69.

11 Aristotle, *The Works*, ed. David Ross, 12 vols (London: Oxford University Press, 1910), IV: HISTORY OF ANIMALS: *Historia Animalium*, 588b.

12 Plato, *The Works: A New and Literal Version, Chiefly from the Text of Stallbaum*, ed. Henry Davis, Bohn's Classical Library, 6 vols (London: George Bell and Sons, 1883), Vol II: *The Republic*; *Timaeus*; *Critias*, 313–409.

13 Arthur O. Lovejoy, *The Great Chain of Being: A Study of the History of an Idea* (Cambridge, MA: Harvard University Press, 1936), 67–98.

14 Jeanne Addison Roberts, 'Animals as Agents of Revelation: The Horizontalizing of the Chain of Being in Shakespeare's Comedies', *New York Literary Forum*, 5–6 (1980): 79–96 (82).

15 Tillyard, *The Elizabethan World Picture*, 34.

16 Egan, *Green Shakespeare: From Ecopolitics to Ecocriticism*, 26–7, 73, 100, 177.

17 Alan B. Shaw, 'Adam and Eve, Paleontology, and the Non-objective Arts', *Journal of Paleontology*, 43 (1969): 1085–98.

18 Jerry Coyne, 'Ernst Mayr and the Origin of Species', *Evolution*, 48 (1994): 19–30.

19 Jody Hey, Robin S. Waples, Michael L. Arnold, Roger K. Butlin and Richard G. Harrison, 'Understanding and Confronting Species Uncertainty in Biology and Conservation', *Trends in Ecology and Evolution*, 18 (2003): 597–603.

20 Joan Thirsk, *Horses in Early Modern England: For Service, for Pleasure, for Power*, The Stenton Lectures 11 (Reading: University of Reading, 1978); Peter Edwards, *The Horse Trade of Tudor and Stuart England* (Cambridge: Cambridge University Press, 1988).

21 W. W. Greg, ed., *Henslowe Papers: Being Documents Supplementary to Henslowe's Diary* (London: Bullen, 1907), 118.

22 Charles Edelman, ed., *Shakespeare's Military Language: A Dictionary*, Athlone Shakespeare Dictionary Series (London: Athlone, 2000), 'lance'.

23 MacDonald P. Jackson, 'Shakespeare's *Richard II* and the Anonymous *Thomas of Woodstock*', *Medieval and Renaissance Drama in England*, 14 (2001): 17–65; MacDonald P. Jackson, 'The Date and Authorship of *Thomas of Woodstock*: Evidence and its Interpretation', *Research Opportunities in Medieval and Renaissance Drama*, 46 (2007): 67–100.

24 Anonymous, *The First Part of the Reign of King Richard the Second, or Thomas of Woodstock*, ed. Wilhelmina P. Frijlinck, Malone Society Reprints (London: Malone Society, 1929), 173a.

25 W. J. Lawrence, *Those Nut-cracking Elizabethans: Studies of the Early Theatre and Drama* (London: Argonaut, 1935), 25.

26 Andreas Höfele, *Stage, Stake, and Scaffold: Humans and Animals in Shakespeare's Theatre* (Oxford: Oxford University Press, 2011).

27 Antonio R. Damasio, *Descartes' Error: Emotion, Reason, and the Human Brain* (London: Picador, 1995).

28 Daniel C. Dennett, '"Our Vegetative Soul: The Search for a Reliable Model of the Human Self": Review of Antonio R. Damasio *Descartes' Error: Emotion, Reason, and the Human*

Brain (London: Picador, 1995)', *Times Literary Supplement*, 4821 (25 August 1995): 3–4.

29 Caroline Spurgeon, *Shakespeare's Imagery and What it Tells us* (Cambridge: Cambridge University Press, 1935), 195–9.

30 William Empson, *The Structure of Complex Words* (London: Chatto and Windus, 1951), 175–84.

31 Empson, *The Structure of Complex Words*, 176.

32 Empson, *The Structure of Complex Words*, 183.

33 Empson, *The Structure of Complex Words*, 183.

34 Spurgeon, *Shakespeare's Imagery and What it Tells us*, 101–2.

35 William Shakespeare, *A Midsummer Night's Dream*, ed. Stanley Wells, New Penguin Shakespeare (Harmondsworth: Penguin, 1967), 31.

36 Leonard Tennenhouse, *Power on Display: The Politics of Shakespeare's Genres* (New York: Methuen, 1986), 74.

37 Eric C. Brown, 'Caliban, Columbus, and Canines in *The Tempest*', *Notes and Queries*, 245 (2000): 92–4.

38 Gabriel Egan, 'Ariel's Costume in the Original Staging of *The Tempest*', *Theatre Notebook*, 51 (1997): 62–72.

39 Egan, *Green Shakespeare: From Ecopolitics to Ecocriticism*, 148–71.

40 John Madden, *Shakespeare in Love*, Motion Picture. Bedford Falls/Miramax/Universal, 1998.

41 Gail Kern Paster, *Humoring the Body: Emotions and the Shakespearean Stage* (Chicago, IL: University of Chicago Press, 2004).

42 Bruce R. Smith, 'E/loco/com/motion', in *From Script to Stage in Early Modern England*, eds. Peter Holland and Stephen Orgel, Redefining British Theatre History (Basingstoke: Palgrave Macmillan, 2004), 131–50 (135–6).

43 Stanley Wells, 'The Failure of *The Two Gentlemen of Verona*', *Shakespeare Jahrbuch*, 99 (1963): 161–73.

44 John Calvin, *Sermons on the Fifth Book of Moses Called Deuteronomy, Translated Out of French By Arthur Golding*, STC 4442 (London: Henry Middleton for George Bishop, 1583), F5r.

45 R. W. Dent, *Shakespeare's Proverbial Language: An Index* (Berkeley: University of California Press, 1981), D506.

46 Joan Fitzpatrick, *Shakespeare and the Language of Food*, Arden Shakespeare Dictionaries (London: Bloomsbury, 2010), 'Crab'.

47 Shakespeare, *Comedies, Histories and Tragedies*, D1v.

48 William Shakespeare, *Hamlet*, eds. Ann Thompson and Neil Taylor, The Arden Shakespeare (London: Thomson Learning, 2006), 2.2.388n.

Chapter 4

1 Egan, *Green Shakespeare: From Ecopolitics to Ecocriticism*, 51–82.

2 S. E. Bengston and A. Dornhaus, 'Be Meek or be Bold? A Colony-level Behavioural Syndrome in Ants', http://dx.doi.org/10.1098/rspb.2014.0518, *Proceedings of the Royal Society B*, 281 (2014): n.p.

3 Paul Baran, 'On Distributed Communications Networks', *Institute of Electrical and Electronic Engineers Transactions on Communications*, 12 (1964): 1–9.

4 Balaji Prabhakar, Katherine N. Dektar and Deborah M. Gordon, 'The Regulation of Ant Colony Foraging Activity Without Spatial Information', *Public Library of Science (PLoS) Computational Biology*, 8.8 (2012): n.p.

5 Dawkins, *The Selfish Gene*, 189–201.

6 Gurr, *The Shakespearean Stage, 1574–1642*, 122–3.

7 Tribble, *Cognition in the Globe: Attention and Memory in Shakespeare's Theatre*.

8 R. A. Foakes and R. T. Rickert, eds, *Henslowe's Diary, Edited with Supplementary Material, Introduction and Notes* (Cambridge: Cambridge University Press, 1961), 308.

9 Tiffany Stern, '"A Small-beer Health to His Second Day": Playwrights, Prologues, and First Performances in the Early Modern Theater', *Studies in Philology*, 101 (2004): 172–99.

10 Michael Warren, 'The Perception of Error: The Editing and the Performance of the Opening of *Coriolanus*', in *Textual Performances: The Modern Reproduction of Shakespeare's Drama*, eds Lukas Erne and Margaret Jane Kidnie (Cambridge: Cambridge University Press, 2004), 127–42.

11 William Shakespeare, *Coriolanus*, ed. Peter Holland, The Arden Shakespeare (London: Bloomsbury, 2013), 95–6.

12 Shakespeare, *Coriolanus*, 82.

13 William Shakespeare, *Julius Caesar*, ed. David Daniell, The Arden Shakespeare (Walton-on-Thames: Thomas Nelson, 1998), 103–4.

14 Anthony Munday, Henry Chettle, Edmund Tilney, Hand C. Thomas, Thomas Dekker, Thomas Heywood and William Shakespeare, *Sir Thomas More*, ed. John Jowett, The Arden Shakespeare (London: Methuen, 2011), 428.

15 Munday, Chettle, Tilney, Thomas, Dekker, Heywood and Shakespeare, *Sir Thomas More*, 6.71n.

16 Paul Menzer, 'The Tragedians of the City? Q1 *Hamlet* and the Settlements of the, 1590s', *Shakespeare Quarterly*, 57 (2006): 162–82 (169–72).

17 Janette Dillon, *Theatre, Court and City, 1595–1610: Drama and Social Space in London* (Cambridge: Cambridge University Press, 2000).

18 William Shakespeare, [*Richard Duke of York*] *The True Tragedie of Richard Duke of Yorke, and the Death of Good King Henrie the Sixt*, STC 21006 BEPD 138a (O) (London: P[eter] S[hort] for Thomas Millington, 1595), A2r, A3r.

19 Scott McMillin and Sally-Beth MacLean, *The Queen's Men and Their Plays* (Cambridge: Cambridge University Press, 1998), 18–36.

20 Karl Marx, *Value, Price and Profit: Addressed to Working Men*, ed. Eleanor Marx Aveling (London: George Allen and Unwin, 1899), 61.

21 Nancy Chodorow, *The Reproduction of Mothering: Psychoanalysis and the Sociology of Gender* (Berkeley: University of California Press, 1978), 7.

22 Herbert A. Simon, 'The Architecture of Complexity',

Proceedings of the American Philosophical Society, 106 (1962): 467–82 (467).

23 Simon, 'The Architecture of Complexity', 468.

24 William Shakespeare, *King Richard II*, ed. Peter Ure, The Arden Shakespeare (London: Methuen, 1956), 5.3.52n.

25 Simon, 'The Architecture of Complexity', 476–7.

26 Erne, *Shakespeare as Literary Dramatist*.

27 Erne, *Shakespeare and the Book Trade*.

28 Hugh Craig and Arthur F. Kinney, *Shakespeare, Computers, and the Mystery of Authorship* (Cambridge: Cambridge University Press, 2009), 40–78.

29 Andrew Gurr, 'Stephano's Leather Bottle', *Notes and Queries*, 257 (2012): 549–50.

30 Erne, *Shakespeare and the Book Trade*, 194–232.

Conclusion

1 Dawkins, *The Selfish Gene*, 193.

2 C. P. Snow, *The Two Cultures and the Scientific Revolution: The Rede Lecture, 1959* (Cambridge: Cambridge University Press, 1959), 14.

3 James Gleick, *The Information: A History, a Theory, a Flood* (New York: Pantheon, 2011).

4 Shakespeare, *Comedies, Histories and Tragedies*, A1r.

BIBLIOGRAPHY

Anonymous *The First Part of the Reign of King Richard the Second, or Thomas of Woodstock*. Ed. Wilhelmina P. Frijlinck. Malone Society Reprints (London: Malone Society, 1929)

Aristotle *The Works*. Ed. David Ross. Vol. 4: HISTORY OF ANIMALS: *Historia Animalium*. 12 vols (London: Oxford University Press, 1910)

Baran, Paul 'On Distributed Communications Networks', *Institute of Electrical and Electronic Engineers Transactions on Communications*, 12 (1964): 1–9

Bate, Jonathan 'Shakespeare's Foolosophy' In *Shakespeare Performed: Essays in Honor of R. A. Foakes*. Ed. Grace Ioppolo (Newark: University of Delaware Press, 2000), 17–32

Bate, Jonathan *The Song of the Earth* (London: Picador, 2000)

Bengston, S. E. and A. Dornhaus 'Be Meek or be Bold? A Colony-level Behavioural Syndrome in Ants'. http://dx.doi.org/10.1098/rspb.2014.0518. *Proceedings of the Royal Society B*, 281 (2014): n.p.

Benjamin, Walter *Illuminations*. Ed. Hannah Arendt. Trans. Harry Zohn (London: Fontana, 1992)

Blayney, Peter W. M. *The First Folio of Shakespeare* (Washington, DC: Folger Library Publications, 1991)

Bloom, Harold *The Western Canon: The Books and School of the Ages* (New York: Harcourt Brace, 1994)

Boehrer, Bruce *Shakespeare Among the Animals: Nature and Society in the Drama of Early Modern England*. Early Modern Cultural Studies (Basingstoke: Palgrave, 2002)

Boehrer, Bruce *Animal Characters: Nonhuman Beings in Early Modern Literature* (Philadelphia: University of Pennsylvania Press, 2010)

Boehrer, Bruce *Environmental Degradation in Jacobean Drama* (Cambridge: Cambridge University Press, 2013)

Borlik, Todd A. *Ecocriticism and Early Modern English Literature:*

Green Pastures. Routledge Studies in Renaissance Literature and Culture 16 (New York: Routledge, 2011)

Branagh, Kenneth *Hamlet*. Motion Picture. Turner/Castle Rock/Columbia/Fishmonger, 1996

Brayton, Dan *Shakespeare's Ocean: An Ecocritical Exploration*. Under the Sign of Nature: Explorations in Ecocriticism (Charlottesville, VA: University of Virginia Press, 2012)

Brockbank, J. P. 'The Frame of Disorder: *Henry VI*' In *Early Shakespeare*. Ed. John Russell Brown and Bernard Harris. Stratford-upon-Avon Studies 3 (London: Edward Arnold, 1961), 73–99

Brooks, Douglas A., ed. *Printing and Parenting in Early Modern England*. Women and Gender in the Early Modern World (Aldershot: Ashgate, 2005)

Brown, Eric C. 'Caliban, Columbus, and Canines in *The Tempest*', *Notes and Queries*, 245 (2000): 92–4

Brown, Georgia 'Defining Nature Through Monstrosity in *Othello* and *Macbeth*' In *Early Modern Ecostudies: From the Florentine Codex to Shakespeare*. Eds. Thomas Hallock, Ivo Kamps and Karen L. Raber. Early Modern Cultural Studies (New York: Palgrave Macmillan, 2008), 55–76

Butterfield, Herbert *The Whig Interpretation of History* (London: G. Bell, 1931)

Calvin, John *Sermons on the Fifth Book of Moses Called Deuteronomy, Translated Out of French By Arthur Golding*. STC 4442 (London: Henry Middleton for George Bishop, 1583)

Carey, Nessa *The Epigenetics Revolution: How Modern Biology is Rewriting Our Understanding of Genetics, Disease and Inheritance* (London: Icon, 2011)

Chapman, George *The Widow's Tears*. STC 4994 BEPD 301a (London: [William Stansby] for John Browne, 1612)

Chapman, George *The Widow's Tears*. Ed. Akihiro Yamada. Revels Plays (London: Methuen, 1975)

Chodorow, Nancy *The Reproduction of Mothering: Psychoanalysis and the Sociology of Gender* (Berkeley: University of California Press, 1978)

Cless, Downing *Ecology and Environment in European Drama*. Advances in Theatre and Performance Studies 14 (New York: Routledge, 2010)

Commoner, Barry *The Closing Circle: Confronting the Environmental Crisis* (New York: Knopf, 1971)

Coyne, Jerry 'Ernst Mayr and the Origin of Species', *Evolution*, 48 (1994): 19–30

Craig, Hugh and Arthur F. Kinney *Shakespeare, Computers, and the Mystery of Authorship* (Cambridge: Cambridge University Press, 2009)

Daly, Martin and Margo Wilson *Homicide*. Foundations of Human Behavior (New York: Aldine de Gruyter, 1988)

Daly, Martin and Margo Wilson *The Truth About Cinderella: A Darwinian View of Parental Love*. Darwinism Today (London: Weidenfeld and Nicolson, 1998)

Damasio, Antonio R. *Descartes' Error: Emotion, Reason, and the Human Brain* (London: Picador, 1995)

Darnton, Robert *The Great Cat Massacre and Other Episodes in French Cultural History* (Harmondsworth: Penguin, 1985)

Dawkins, Richard *The Selfish Gene* (Oxford: Oxford University Press, 1976)

Dawkins, Richard *The Extended Phenotype: The Gene as the Unit of Selection* (Oxford: Oxford University Press, 1982)

Dawkins, Richard *The Blind Watchmaker*, 2nd edn (London: Penguin, 1991)

Dawkins, Richard *The Extended Phenotype: The Long Reach of the Gene*, 2nd edn with a new foreword by Daniel Dennett (Oxford: Oxford University Press, 1999)

De Waal, Frans B. M. *Chimpanzee Politics: Power and Sex Among Apes* (London: Cape, 1982)

De Waal, Frans B. M. *The Ape and the Sushi Master: Cultural Reflections By a Primatologist* (London: Allen Lane, 2001)

Dennett, Daniel C. *The Intentional Stance* (Cambridge, MA: MIT Press, 1987)

Dennett, Daniel C. '"Our Vegetative Soul: The Search for a Reliable Model of the Human Self": Review of Antonio R. Damasio *Descartes' Error: Emotion, Reason, and the Human Brain* (London: Picador, 1995)'. *Times Literary Supplement*, 4821 (25 August 1995): 3–4

Dennett, Daniel C. 'How Has Darwin's Theory of Natural Selection Transformed Our View of Humanity's Place in the Universe?', 7th edn In *Life: The Science of Biology*, II: Evolution, Diversity, and Ecology. Eds William K. Purves, David Sadava, Gordon H.

Orians and H. Craig Heller (Sunderland, MA: Sinauer, 2003), 523

Dent, R. W. *Shakespeare's Proverbial Language: An Index* (Berkeley: University of California Press, 1981)

Dillon, Janette *Theatre, Court and City, 1595–1610: Drama and Social Space in London* (Cambridge: Cambridge University Press, 2000)

Eagleton, Terry *Literary Theory: An Introduction* (Oxford: Basil Blackwell, 1983)

Eagleton, Terry *Ideology: An Introduction* (London: Verso, 1991)

Edelman, Charles, ed. *Shakespeare's Military Language: A Dictionary*. Athlone Shakespeare Dictionary Series (London: Athlone, 2000)

Edwards, Peter *The Horse Trade of Tudor and Stuart England* (Cambridge: Cambridge University Press, 1988)

Egan, Gabriel 'Ariel's Costume in the Original Staging of *The Tempest*', *Theatre Notebook*, 51 (1997): 62–72

Egan, Gabriel *Shakespeare and Marx*. Oxford Shakespeare Topics (Oxford: Oxford University Press, 2004)

Egan, Gabriel *Green Shakespeare: From Ecopolitics to Ecocriticism*. Accents on Shakespeare (London: Routledge, 2006)

Egan, Gabriel *The Struggle for Shakespeare's Text: Twentieth-century Editorial Theory and Practice* (Cambridge: Cambridge University Press, 2010)

Egan, Gabriel 'Gaia and the Great Chain of Being' In *Ecocritical Shakespeare*. Eds Lynne Bruckner and Daniel Brayton. Literary and Scientific Cultures of Early Modernity (Aldershot: Ashgate, 2011), 57–69

Empson, William *The Structure of Complex Words* (London: Chatto and Windus, 1951)

Erne, Lukas *Shakespeare as Literary Dramatist* (Cambridge: Cambridge University Press, 2003)

Erne, Lukas *Shakespeare and the Book Trade* (Cambridge: Cambridge University Press, 2013)

Estok, Simon C. *Ecocriticism and Shakespeare: Reading Ecophobia*. Literatures, Cultures, and Environment (New York: Palgrave Macmillan, 2011)

Fill, Alwin 'Ecolinguistics: The State of the Art, 1998' In *The Ecolinguistics Reader: Language, Ecology and Environment*.

Eds. Alwin Fill and Peter Mühlhäusler (London: Continuum, 2001), 43–53

Fitzpatrick, Joan *Shakespeare and the Language of Food.* Arden Shakespeare Dictionaries (London: Bloomsbury, 2010)

Foakes, R. A. and R. T. Rickert, eds *Henslowe's Diary, Edited with Supplementary Material, Introduction and Notes* (Cambridge: Cambridge University Press, 1961)

Fudge, Erica *Perceiving Animals: Humans and Beasts in Early Modern English Culture* (Basingstoke: Macmillan, 2000)

Fudge, Erica *Brutal Reasoning: Animals, Rationality, and Humanity in Early Modern England* (Ithaca, NY: Cornell University Press, 2006)

Gajowski, Evelyn, ed, *Presentism, Gender, and Sexuality in Shakespeare* (Basingstoke: Palgrave Macmillan, 2008)

Garber, Marjorie *Shakespeare's Ghost Writers: Literature as Uncanny Causality* (London: Methuen, 1987)

Geertz, Clifford *The Interpretation of Cultures* (New York: Basic Books, 1973)

Gleick, James *The Information: A History, a Theory, a Flood* (New York: Pantheon, 2011)

Glotfelty, Cheryll 'Introduction: Literary Studies in an Age of Environmental Crisis' In *The Ecocriticism Reader: Landmarks in Literary Ecology.* Eds Cheryll Glotfelty and Harold Fromm (Athens, GA: University of Georgia Press, 1996), xv–xxxvii

Gower, John *Confessio Amantis*, STC 12142 (London: William Caxton, 1493 [actually, 1483])

Gower, John *Confessio Amantis*, STC 12143 (London: Thomas Berthelette, 1532)

Gower, John *Confessio Amantis*, STC 12144 (London: Thomas Berthelette, 1554)

Grady, Hugh and Terence Hawkes, eds *Presentist Shakespeares.* Accents on Shakespeare (London: Routledge, 2007)

Greenblatt, Stephen *Renaissance Self-fashioning: From More to Shakespeare* (Chicago, IL: University of Chicago Press, 1980)

Greg, W. W., ed. *Henslowe Papers: Being Documents Supplementary to Henslowe's Diary* (London: Bullen, 1907)

Gurr, Andrew *The Shakespearean Stage, 1574–1642*, 3rd edn (Cambridge: Cambridge University Press, 1992)

Gurr, Andrew 'Stephano's Leather Bottle', *Notes and Queries*, 257 (2012): 549–50

Höfele, Andreas *Stage, Stake, and Scaffold: Humans and Animals in Shakespeare's Theatre* (Oxford: Oxford University Press, 2011)

Hadfield, Andrew *Shakespeare and Republicanism* (Cambridge: Cambridge University Press, 2005)

Hamilton, W. D. 'The Genetical Evolution of Social Behaviour [Part] I' *Journal of Theoretical Biology*, 7 (1964): 1–16

Hamilton, W. D. 'The Genetical Evolution of Social Behaviour [Part] II', *Journal of Theoretical Biology*, 7 (1964), 17–52

Hawkes, Terence *Shakespeare in the Present*. Accents on Shakespeare (London: Routledge, 2002)

Hey, Jody, Robin S. Waples, Michael L. Arnold, Roger K. Butlin and Richard G. Harrison 'Understanding and Confronting Species Uncertainty in Biology and Conservation', *Trends in Ecology and Evolution*, 18 (2003): 597–603

Hiltner, Ken *What Else is Pastoral?: Renaissance Literature and the Environment* (Ithaca, NY: Cornell University Press, 2011)

Holland, Peter 'Feasting and Starving: Staging Food in Shakespeare', *Shakespeare Jahrbuch*, 145 (2009): 11–28

Honigmann, E. A. J. 'How Happy Was Shakespeare with the Printed Versions of His Plays?', *Modern Language Review*, 105 (2010): 937–51

Hosley, Richard 'Was There a Music-room in Shakespeare's Globe?', *Shakespeare Survey*, 13 (1960): 113–23

Huston, John *The African Queen*. Motion Picture. Romulus Films/ Horizon Pictures, 1951

Ingram, William *The Business of Playing: The Beginnings of the Adult Professional Theater in Elizabethan England* (Ithaca, NY: Cornell University Press, 1992)

Ingram, William 'The "Evolution" of the Elizabethan Playing Company' In *The Development of Shakespeare's Theater*. Ed. John H. Astington. AMS Studies in the Renaissance 24 (New York: AMS, 1992), 13–28

Jackson, MacDonald P. 'Shakespeare's *Richard II* and the Anonymous *Thomas of Woodstock*', *Medieval and Renaissance Drama in England*, 14 (2001): 17–65

Jackson, MacDonald P. *Defining Shakespeare*: Pericles *as Test Case* (Oxford: Oxford University Press, 2003)

Jackson, MacDonald P. 'The Date and Authorship of *Thomas of Woodstock*: Evidence and its Interpretation', *Research*

Opportunities in Medieval and Renaissance Drama, 46 (2007), 67–100

Keenan, Siobhan and Peter Davidson 'The Iconography of the Globe' In *Shakespeare's Globe Rebuilt*. Eds. J. R. Mulryne, Margaret Shewring and Andrew Gurr (Cambridge: Cambridge University Press, 1997), 147–56

Knight, G. Wilson *The Crown of Life: Essays in Interpretation of Shakespeare's Final Plays* (Oxford: Oxford University Press, 1947)

Knight, Leah *Reading Green in Early Modern England* (Burlington, VT: Ashgate, 2013)

Lamarck, Jean-Baptiste *Zoological Philosophy: An Exposition with Regard to the Natural History of Animals*. Translated and introduced by Hugh Elliot (London: Macmillan, 1914)

Laroche, Rebecca 'Ophelia's Plants and the Death of Violets' In *Ecocritical Shakespeare*. Eds. Lynne Bruckner and Dan Brayton. Literary and Scientific Cultures of Early Modernity (Aldershot: Ashgate, 2011), 211–21

Laurence, Anne *Women in England, 1500–1760: A Social History* (London: Weidenfeld and Nicolson, 1994)

Lawrence, W. J. *Those Nut-cracking Elizabethans: Studies of the Early Theatre and Drama* (London: Argonaut, 1935)

Lenton, Timothy M. 'Gaia and Natural Selection', doi:10.1038/28792 *Nature*, 394 (1998): 439–47

Lesser, Zachary and Peter Stallybrass 'The First Literary *Hamlet* and the Commonplacing of Professional Plays', *Shakespeare Quarterly*, 59 (2008): 371–420

Locke, John *An Essay Concerning Human Understanding*. Wing L2738 (London: Elizabeth Holt for Thomas Basset, 1690)

Lovejoy, Arthur O. *The Great Chain of Being: A Study of the History of an Idea* (Cambridge, MA: Harvard University Press, 1936)

Lovelock, James E. 'Daisy World: A Cybernetic Proof of the Gaia Hypothesis', *Coevolution Quarterly*, 38 (1983): 66–72

Lovelock, James E. 'Reflections on Gaia' In *Scientists Debate Gaia: The Next Century*. Eds. Stephen H. Schneider, James R. Miller, Eileen Crist and Penelope J. Boston (Cambridge, MA: Massachusetts Institute of Technology Press, 2004), 1–5

Lovelock, James E. *The Revenge of Gaia: Why the Earth is Fighting*

Back and How we Can Still Save Humanity (London: Penguin, 2006)

Madden, John *Shakespeare in Love*. Motion Picture. Bedford Falls/Miramax/Universal, 1998

Margulis, Lynn *Origin of Eukaryotic Cells* (New Haven, CT: Yale University Press, 1971)

Markley, Robert 'Summer's Lease: Shakespeare in the Little Ice Age' In *Early Modern Ecostudies: From the Florentine Codex to Shakespeare*. Eds. Thomas Hallock, Ivo Kamps and Karen L. Raber. Early Modern Cultural Studies (New York: Palgrave Macmillan, 2008), 131–42

Marx, Karl *Value, Price and Profit: Addressed to Working Men*. Ed. Eleanor Marx Aveling (London: George Allen and Unwin, 1899)

Masten, Jeffrey *Textual Intercourse: Collaboration, Authorship, and Sexualities in Renaissance Drama*. Cambridge Studies in Renaissance Literature and Culture 14 (Cambridge: Cambridge University Press, 1997)

McColley, Diane Kelsey *Poetry and Ecology in the Age of Milton and Marvell*. Literary and Scientific Cultures of Early Modernity (Aldershot: Ashgate, 2007)

McMillin, Scott and Sally-Beth MacLean *The Queen's Men and Their Plays* (Cambridge: Cambridge University Press, 1998)

Mentz, Steve 'Strange Weather in *King Lear*', *Shakespeare*, 6 (2010): 139–52

Mentz, Steve 'Shakespeare's Beach House, or the Green and the Blue in *Macbeth*', *Shakespeare Studies*, 39 (2011): 84–93

Menzer, Paul 'The Tragedians of the City? Q1 *Hamlet* and the Settlements of the 1590s', *Shakespeare Quarterly*, 57 (2006): 162–82

Munday, Anthony, Henry Chettle, Edmund Tilney, Hand C. Thomas, Thomas Dekker, Thomas Heywood and William Shakespeare *Sir Thomas More*. Ed. John Jowett. The Arden Shakespeare (London: Methuen, 2011)

Nardizzi, Vin 'Shakespeare's Globe and England's Woods', *Shakespeare Studies*, 39 (2011): 54–63

O'Dair, Sharon 'Slow Shakespeare: An Eco-critique of "Method" in Early Modern Literary Studies'. In *Early Modern Ecostudies: From the Florentine Codex to Shakespeare*. Eds. Thomas Hallock, Ivo Kamps and Karen L. Raber. Early Modern Cultural Studies (New York: Palgrave Macmillan, 2008), 11–30

O'Dair, Sharon '"To Fright the Animals and to Kill Them Up":
Shakespeare and Ecology', *Shakespeare Studies*, 39 (2011): 74–83

Paster, Gail Kern *Humoring the Body: Emotions and the
Shakespearean Stage* (Chicago, IL: University of Chicago Press,
2004)

Pinker, Steven *The Blank Slate: The Modern Denial of Human
Nature* (London: Penguin, 2002)

Plato *The Works: A New and Literal Version, Chiefly from the Text
of Stallbaum*. Ed. Henry Davis. Vol. II: *The Republic*; *Timaeus*;
Critias. 6 vols. Bohn's Classical Library (London: George Bell
and Sons, 1883)

Plumwood, Val *Feminism and the Mastery of Nature*. Feminism for
Today (London: Routledge, 1993)

Prabhakar, Balaji, Katherine N. Dektar and Deborah M. Gordon
'The Regulation of Ant Colony Foraging Activity Without
Spatial Information', *Public Library of Science (PLoS)
Computational Biology*, 8.8 (2012): n.p.

Quarshie, Hugh *Second Thoughts About Othello*. International
Shakespeare Association Occasional Papers 7 (Chipping
Campden: International Shakespeare Association, 1999)

Roberts, Jeanne Addison 'Animals as Agents of Revelation:
The Horizontalizing of the Chain of Being in Shakespeare's
Comedies', *New York Literary Forum*, 5–6 (1980): 79–96

Ronayne, John 'Totus Mundus Agit Histrionem [The Whole
World Moves the Actor]: The Interior Decorative Scheme of
the Bankside Globe' In *Shakespeare's Globe Rebuilt*. Eds. J. R.
Mulryne, Margaret Shewring and Andrew Gurr (Cambridge:
Cambridge University Press, 1997), 121–46

Sagan [later Margulis], Lynn 'On the Origin of Mitosing Cells',
Journal of Theoretical Biology, 14 (1967): 225–74

Schneider, Stephen H., James R. Miller, Eileen Crist and Penelope
J. Boston, eds *Scientists Debate Gaia: The Next Century*
(Cambridge MA: Massachusetts Institute of Technology Press,
2004)

Shakespeare, William *[Richard Duke of York] The True Tragedie
of Richard Duke of Yorke, and the Death of Good King Henrie
the Sixt*. STC 21006 BEPD 138a (O) (London: P[eter] S[hort] for
Thomas Millington, 1595)

Shakespeare, William *Comedies, Histories and Tragedies*. STC
22273 (F1) (London: Isaac and William Jaggard for Edward

Blount, John Smethwick, Isaac Jaggard and William Aspley, 1623)

Shakespeare, William *The Works*. Ed. Alexander Pope. Vol. 6: *Troilus and Cressida*; *Cymbeline*; *Romeo and Juliet*; *Hamlet*; *Othello*, 6 vols (London: Jacob Tonson, 1723)

Shakespeare, William *King Richard II*. Ed. Peter Ure. The Arden Shakespeare (London: Methuen, 1956)

Shakespeare, William *A Midsummer Night's Dream*. Ed. Stanley Wells. New Penguin Shakespeare (Harmondsworth: Penguin, 1967)

Shakespeare, William *Julius Caesar*. Ed. David Daniell. The Arden Shakespeare (Walton-on-Thames: Thomas Nelson, 1998)

Shakespeare, William *Pericles*. Ed. Suzanne Gossett. The Arden Shakespeare (London: Thomson Learning, 2004)

Shakespeare, William *The Winter's Tale*. Eds. Robert Kean Turner, Virginia Westling Haas, Robert A. Jones, Andrew J. Sabol and Patricia E. Tatspaugh. The New Variorum Edition of Shakespeare (New York: The Modern Language Association of America, 2005)

Shakespeare, William *Hamlet*. Eds Ann Thompson and Neil Taylor. The Arden Shakespeare (London: Thomson Learning, 2006)

Shakespeare, William *The Winter's Tale*. Ed. John Pitcher. The Arden Shakespeare (London: Methuen, 2010)

Shakespeare, William *Coriolanus*. Ed. Peter Holland. The Arden Shakespeare (London: Bloomsbury, 2013)

Shakespeare, William and George Wilkins *[Pericles] The Late, and Much Admired Play Called Pericles, Prince of Tyre*. STC 22334 BEPD 284a (Q1) (London: [William White and Thomas Creede] for Henry Gosson, 1609)

Shannon, Laurie *The Accommodated Animal: Cosmopolity in Shakespeare's Locales* (Chicago, IL: University of Chicago Press, 2013)

Shaw, Alan B. 'Adam and Eve, Paleontology, and the Non-objective Arts', *Journal of Paleontology*, 43 (1969): 1085–98

Sidney, Philip *The Defence of Poesie*. STC 22535 (London: [Thomas Creede] for William Ponsonby, 1595)

Simon, Herbert A. 'The Architecture of Complexity', *Proceedings of the American Philosophical Society*, 106 (1962): 467–82

Singer, Peter '"Animal Liberation": Review of Stanley Godlovitch, Rosalind Godlovitch, and John Harris, eds *Animals, Men and*

Morals (New York: Taplinger, 1971)', *New York Review of Books*, 20.3 (1973), 17–21

Smith, Bruce R. 'E/loco/com/motion' In *From Script to Stage in Early Modern England*. Eds Peter Holland and Stephen Orgel. Redefining British Theatre History (Basingstoke: Palgrave Macmillan, 2004), 131–50

Smith, Bruce R. *The Key of Green: Passion and Perception in Renaissance Culture* (Chicago, IL: University of Chicago Press, 2009)

Smith, Helen "A Man in Print':? Shakespeare and the Representation of the Press'. Trans. Edward Babcock. In *Shakespeare's Book: Essays in Reading, Writing and Reception*. Eds. Richard Meek, Jane Rickard and Richard Wilson (Manchester: Manchester University Press, 2008), 59–78

Snow, C. P. *The Two Cultures and the Scientific Revolution: The Rede Lecture, 1959* (Cambridge: Cambridge University Press, 1959)

Spurgeon, Caroline *Shakespeare's Imagery and What it Tells us* (Cambridge: Cambridge University Press, 1935)

Stern, Tiffany ' "A Small-beer Health to His Second Day": Playwrights, Prologues, and First Performances in the Early Modern Theater', *Studies in Philology*, 101 (2004): 172–99

Tallis, Raymond *In Defence of Realism* (London: Edward Arnold, 1988)

Tallis, Raymond *Not Saussure: A Critique of Post-Saussurean Literary Theory* (Basingstoke: Macmillan, 1988)

Tallis, Raymond *Theorrhoea and After* (Basingstoke: Macmillan, 1998)

Taylor, Gary 'The Structure of Performance: Act-intervals in the London Theatres, 1576–1642' In *Shakespeare Reshaped, 1606–1623*. Eds. Gary Taylor and John Jowett. Oxford Shakespeare Studies (Oxford: Clarendon Press, 1993), 3–50

Taylor, Gary 'Shakespeare's Midlife Crisis', *Guardian (newspaper)*, 3 May 2004: 11

Tennenhouse, Leonard *Power on Display: The Politics of Shakespeare's Genres* (New York: Methuen, 1986)

Theis, Jeffrey S. *Writing the Forest in Early Modern England: A Sylvan Pastoral Nation*. Medieval and Renaissance Literary Studies (Pittsburgh, PA: Duquesne University Press, 2009)

Thirsk, Joan *Horses in Early Modern England: For Service,*

for Pleasure, for Power. The Stenton Lectures 11 (Reading: University of Reading, 1978)

Thompson, Ann *Shakespeare's Chaucer: A Study in Literary Origins*. Liverpool English Texts and Studies 16 (Liverpool: Liverpool University Press, 1978)

Tillyard, E. M. W. *The Elizabethan World Picture* (London: Chatto and Windus, 1943)

Tillyard, E. M. W. *Shakespeare's History Plays* (London: Chatto and Windus, 1944)

Tribble, Evelyn 'Distributing Cognition in the Globe', *Shakespeare Quarterly*, 56 (2005): 135–55

Tribble, Evelyn *Cognition in the Globe: Attention and Memory in Shakespeare's Theatre*. Cognitive Studies in Literature and Performance (Basingstoke: Palgrave Macmillan, 2011)

Tribble, Evelyn and John Sutton 'Cognitive Ecology as a Framework for Shakespearean Studies', *Shakespeare Studies*, 39 (2011): 94–103

Vickers, Brian *Appropriating Shakespeare: Contemporary Critical Quarrels* (New Haven, CT: Yale University Press, 1993)

Waldron, Jennifer 'Of Stones and Stony Hearts: Desdemona, Hermione, and Post-Reformation Theatre' In *The Indistinct Human in Renaissance Literature*. Eds Jean E. Feerick and Vin Nardizzi. Early Modern Cultural Studies (New York: Palgrave Macmillan, 2012), 205–27

Wall, Wendy 'De-generation: Editions, Offspring, and *Romeo and Juliet*' In *From Performance to Print in Shakespeare's England*. Eds Peter Holland and Stephen Orgel. Redefining British Theatre History 2 (Basingstoke: Palgrave Macmillan, 2006), 152–70

Warren, Michael 'The Perception of Error: The Editing and the Performance of the Opening of *Coriolanus*' In *Textual Performances: The Modern Reproduction of Shakespeare's Drama*. Eds Lukas Erne and Margaret Jane Kidnie (Cambridge: Cambridge University Press, 2004), 127–42

Watson, Robert N. *Back to Nature: The Green and the Real in the Late Renaissance* (Philadelphia: University of Pennsylvania Press, 2006)

Wells, Stanley 'The Failure of *The Two Gentlemen of Verona*', *Shakespeare Jahrbuch*, 99 (1963): 161–73

Wells, Stanley, Gary Taylor, John Jowett and William Montgomery

William Shakespeare: A Textual Companion (Oxford: Oxford University Press, 1987)

Wiggins, Martin *Drama and the Transfer of Power in Renaissance England* (Oxford: Oxford University Press, 2012)

Wilding, Nick '"The Strangest Piece of News": Review of David Wootton *Watcher of the Skies* (New Haven CT: Yale University Press, 2010) and J. L. Heilbron *Galileo* (Oxford: Oxford University Press, 2010)', *London Review of Books*, 33.11 (2 June 2014), 31–2

Williams, Raymond *The Country and the City* (London: Chatto and Windus, 1973)

Wootton, David '"Traffic of the Mind – Facts, Theories, Theories of Facts": The Scientific Revolution and a Forty Year Struggle Not to be Confined By Yesterday's Questions', Review of Robert S. Westman *The Copernican Question: Prognostication, Skepticism, and Celestial Order* (Berkeley: University of California Press, 2011), and Steven Shapin and Simon Schaffer *Leviathan and the Air-pump: Hobbes, Boyle, and the Experimental Life*, New edn (Princeton, NJ: Princeton University Press, 2011), *Times Literary Supplement* 5664 (21 October 2011): 3–5

Zeffirelli, Franco *Hamlet*. Motion Picture. Warner/Le Studio Canal+/Carolco/Icon/Marquis/Nelson, 1990

INDEX